HALI`A of HAWAI`I
A LEGACY of LANGUAGE

A Memoir by

Frances Nelson Frazier

with *SPECIAL ADDITION*
Capt. Richard Nelson's *Diary & Ships' Log* (CONDENSED)

For the enjoyment of Helen and Marcia, me ke aloha pu

authorHOUSE®

AuthorHouse™
1663 Liberty Drive
Bloomington, IN 47403
www.authorhouse.com
Phone: 1-800-839-8640

First published by AuthorHouse 3/18/2010

ISBN: 978-1-4490-7709-9 (e)
ISBN: 978-1-4490-7708-2 (sc)

Library of Congress Control Number: 2010901348

Printed in the United States of America
Bloomington, Indiana

This book is printed on acid-free paper.

This book is a work of heart and mind
published independently
because it is meant to come into being,
with no grant support from national or state agencies,
non-profit organizations or private patrons.

TropicBird Press

Published concurrently on Kaua`i & Distributed in Hawai`i by
TropicBird Press, 5753 Noni St., Kapa`a,
Hawai`i 96746-9659, U.S.A.
www.tropicbirdpress.net

In memory of my husband

Hal

July 29, 1911 – March 15, 2004

with fond recollection,

Hali`a

*H*ALI`A of *H*AWAI`I
A LEGACY of LANGUAGE

A Memoir

*"Once in a while we are given glimpses of a pathway
on which we are seemingly guided from childhood,
and happy is the person who is able to follow the pathway that is offered,
because those are the people who can accept themselves as they are."*
– Frances N. Frazier

CONTENTS

PREFACE

EDITOR'S NOTES

Frances calls me about the dedication of this book, voices concern because she is getting "sketchy." She laughs when I say, "Sketchy, but lovable."

Last time we talked about finalizing the order of the chapters, she said I "could have my way with her." Always, there is this note of humor to offset the deep and dreaded concern that her ability to remember fine details–but mostly faces, and voices–is slowly leaving her, that at times, a cocoon of haze and forgetting is beginning to envelop her

The woman who is a Living Treasure sits in her favorite reading chair, several of her favorite mysteries at hand on the hammered brass tray from Dacca, a ray of sunshine lighting the bobbed thatch of soft, white hair, a Līhu'e breeze cooling her through the screen doorway of her new apartment. Close by lies Meali'ili'i, the small, intelligent dog-who-believes-she-is-a-human and remains a constant shadow and companion to "Aunty Hali'a"–Frances Frazier–since "Uncle Hal" is gone. Sometimes when I find them, Frances and Mea (for short) are walking about the manicured green grass of the new apartment complex, in perfect accord.

Some years before Frances came with her *hānai* daughter Kathy Valier to a writers meeting to read from the Dacca chapters of this work, I was deeply moved by Frances' presentation of an historical overview of the epic story of "Ko'olau the Leper" for an Elderhostel travel-and-learn group I led, given through the auspices of Hawai'i Pacific University. I had heard of her work of translating this story of Kaluaiko'olau, "the leper" who defied the dictates and rules of the Provisional Government of Hawai'i in the late 1800s and disappeared into Kaua'i's Kalalau Valley with his wife and child. In the 1980s, a copy of her translation published in the Hawai'i Journal of History had come into my hands by way of her neighbor in Ōma'o, a friend who knew my interests. About that time I heard that Frances, in her casual, comfortable way of wearing shorts well after the age of fifty, was a role model for another friend, who with her husband had looked over the Kapahi property Frances and Hal were selling before moving to Ōma'o. I also noticed "Frances N. Frazier" signed to many well-taken and thoughtful letters on various issues of growth and expansion published in "The Forum" letters-to-the-editor section of The Garden Island, the local newspaper.

I began to respect and like the name of Frances N. Frazier and what it stood for before I met and came to love the down-to-earth, intriguing and very caring woman behind it, before I learned that we shared a connection with India, never thinking I would at some point be given the honor of editing and publishing her life story, a story that has become this book, Hali'a, A Legacy of Language. Like all literary and visual works, there exists an interesting story-behind-the-story (as yet, unwritten).

Each reader of Hali'a will note the wide, relative historical time span of a long and bountiful life. In "chanting her genealogy" in the opening chapters, the author pushes the years back even further. Coming forward, we move from sailing ships through "flying boats" to jet airplanes in sequence, along with Frances' stories of her sea captain father and portions of his own diary and ships' log embedded at the end of her own story, how life events led her to discovery of the Hawaiian language, a blood legacy, and how she became adept at translation and left her own legacy of important work. We also hear impressions of an earlier time and style of life on O'ahu, work, marriage and family life set before and after the traumatic events of Pearl Harbor and World War II. We learn of the joy of an inquiring mind expanding and questioning with the opportunities that came for travel in fabled places and residency abroad, and resultant contrast and comparison with home and different cultural ways in Hawai'i.

My hope is that this book that comes from her written memoir and collected papers and letters will come to grace that centerpiece table in her living room, just as it will come "home" to its many readers, who will appreciate the importance of the individuality of Aunty Hali'a's life story–an 'olelo spanning close to one hundred years. The memoir reflects the experiences of one daughter of Hawai'i in another gentler time, as well as the multiple touch points that take her unique story into the Hawai'i of today and includes world travels; by its very individuality, this memoir offers a universal connection with people, their sensibilities, and places around the globe.

Frances Frazier has lived an amazing ninety-five years to date, a life that began fourteen years after Hawai'i became a Territory of the United States of America, and now in 2009 encompasses the commemoration of fifty years of Statehood. Her memoir is an account of a *pono* life of trust in its many decades as they unfolded, bringing her an important work to be done here in Hawai'i that became entwined with her interest in learning and correctly translating the Hawaiian language, especially as it related to land deeds that could influence the making and breaking of rights to the *'āina*, the land, for people of Hawaiian heritage.

Granted, being in the right place at the right time, being just who she was with a particular consciousness and set of talents, and being open to the people she met and worked with, and with whom she became bonded for life, all of these parts merge in the telling of the serendipity of that journey.

Serendipity has continued to light the way as this manuscript and graphics, and the special addition of the author's father's "Diary and Ships' Log" were readied for publication. Heartfelt *mahalos* to thank all who have helped in support of the exacting process which became, at times, a treasure hunt–and find: First of all, Frances Frazier, herself; daughter Stephanie Frazier; Hawai'i State Archives; editorial support from Kathy Valier; Anita Manning; Noni Garner; Delano "Dee" Kawahara, the other wing of the TropicBird; readers Sally Jo Manea, Fernando Peñalosa (who also advised on Arabic language), Wil Welsh; the Kaua'i Writers Group; Joy Jobson; photographer Dana Edmunds and Ginger Edmunds; photo-journalist Anne O'Malley; Noelani Lee and the Dudoit family of Moloka'i; T. Scott Cunningham, Commercial Harbors Manager, Honolulu, and Design Engineers; Deborah Kuwaye, Department of Transportation, Harbors Division, Honolulu; Edwin Finney, Jr., Curator Branch, Photographic Section, Naval History and Heritage Command, WA, D.C.; Frank Arre, Naval Historical Foundation–Photo Service, WA, D.C.; Lisa Aguilar and Paul Rascoe, Research Services Division, University of Texas Libraries, The University of Texas at Austin; Research Services, The

Purdue Library, Donald H. Dyal Ship Collection; Naomi Sodetani; Leigh Morrison, *"Hana Hou"* Magazine, Hawaiian Airlines; Nancy J. Budd, Atty.-at-Law. Also, at AuthorHouse during production of this book's manuscript, Silvia Panigada and her Team Tigris. And all those beings mentioned in this work, no longer of this earth, but still present with us.

Please note that in this book we have elected to use italics for Hawaiian words, and the diacritical markings for the `okina, or glottal stop ( `) and the *kahakō,* macron (‾). The exception for this guide to pronunciation is in some proper names and in quotations from the *Baibala Hemolele,* Hawaiian Bible, and other works, such as the condensed version of the Diary and Ships' Log of Richard Nelson, where such markings were not used.

Also, we hope readers will enjoy in this Preface, letters from the author's daughter and *hānai,* unofficially adopted "daughters." We decided their memories should lead, rather than follow the memoir, to present various glimpses and snatches of time that may lend echoes and reflections as Frances' own story unfolds.

Dawn Fraser Kawahara
Wailua, Kaua`i, Hawai`i
October, 2009

LETTERS from THREE
HĀNAI DAUGHTERS

Noni Garner, Anita Manning, and Kathy Valier are adult "daughters" the author and her husband informally adopted and by whom they were, in turn, loved and honored. Each of these three women became close and were brought into the family circle at various times, sometimes when the Fraziers' own daughter Stephanie was working and living far from home and they were without family close by.

Following are accounts of how the relationships developed and flourished as shared in the present day by the three *hānai* daughters.

Noni Garner

My mother Vivian Desha and Frances met each other in the mid-1930s when they were just beginning their careers in Honolulu and they remained fast friends until my mother's death in 1981. It seemed natural for each to become godparents to the children of the other.

Our two families remained close. Some of my warmest childhood memories are the meals we shared together. Hal, Frances' husband, would throw lobsters on the barbecue at the house in Nu'uanu Valley while Stephanie, their daughter, and I ran and slid through the muddy forest that was their backyard to the river for a swim. Or our families would meet at the Frazier's Lanikai house, my mother bringing the makings of a meal (vegetables, chicken, beef, but never pork, just in case Pele was near as we drove over the Pali). The kids swam, trying hard to avoid the jellyfish and men o' war, while Frances and my mother cooked and chatted and my dad and Hal exchanged views on the latest news. The meals were always delicious and we left happy and replete.

Always a part of the household were the animals that gave Frances such great delight. Sweet-natured German shepherds. Alert parakeets. The occasional poi dog from the Humane Society. The rescued bird whose singing heralded the day. And her horses, which gave her such pleasure, were worth, as she has said, the back distress riding eventually caused.

And I remember Hal. Hal, so in love with his wife, but who, with his imposing frame, shining bald head, and booming deep, gruff voice terrified me as a child. Frances, soft-spoken and patient, mediated my experience of Hal, until, as I grew older, I developed my own relationship with him. I so looked forward to seeing them on my visits from the mainland where I established myself after high school. Their home was always open to me, and I remember fondly whiling away hours playing cribbage with Hal, talking story, while Frances worked at her translations in the next room.

Frances has been sensitive to my interest in the Hawaiian language and culture although my life on the mainland has served to distance me from my native state and history. She has always been kind in answering my questions and sharing her knowledge and took it upon herself to send me separately, a year before its publication, a copy of her introduction to her translation of the book *Kamehameha and His Warrior Kekūhaupi'o*, which discussed at length the life and contributions of Stephen Langhern Desha, Sr., my great uncle. I had known little about him and was so pleased to be able think about my family in light of his life and contributions.

My mother gave me many things, but her greatest gift was the presence in my life of her friends. Frances has always been steady and caring, validating my link with the land I love, confirming my welcome whenever I wish to return. I am so grateful.

September, 2009
San Rafael, California

About Noni Garner: Born in Honolulu, she attended Kamehameha Elementary and Punahou Schools, where she played flute in the band. Upon graduation in 1966, she moved to the Mainland for college, changing majors regularly and taking long breaks to consider career options. After receiving a Bachelor of Arts degree in Humanities from the University of California at Berkeley in 1986, she worked as a residential real estate sales agent before being hired by a bank trust department to manage its real estate portfolio, a job that became a profession Noni says she still finds to be fun and satisfying after fifteen years.

She continues to play flute and piccolo for pleasure in chamber music groups and community orchestras. She looks forward to the passionate exchange of ideas as a member of a book club, and enjoys hiking the mountains of Northern California with friends and her recent discovery-kayaking. This hānai daughter of Frances Frazier says, "Although I have a wonderful life in California, I miss Hawai`i and return regularly to visit family and friends."

~ ~ ~

Anita Manning

Frances and Hal (Harold) Frazier became my *hānai*, or surrogate parents by a slow process of growing together. A few days after Labor Day 1969, I came to Hawai`i and the Bishop Museum–for nine months. I came as a National Endowment for the Humanities intern and stayed at the Museum for twenty-six years.

At the Bishop Museum, I spent my first month or more moving from department to department. The idea was to understand what all the units did and their functions in a museum. Eventually, I ended up dividing my time between two areas: the Registrar's Office and the Education Department, which at that time meant the Planetarium. George Bunton ran the Planetarium and managed a list of lecturers, including Louis Valier [father of Frances and Hal Frazier's surrogate daughter Kathy Valier]. George's wife Marie Bunton split the reception, ticket taking, and clerical jobs with Frances Frazier. Marie and Frances "adopted" me, explaining Hawai`i and life! Over the years, the mother-daughter relationship grew: I began sending both Marie and Frances Mother's Day cards, for example. We each filled a place in the other's life.

On a professional level, as an intern I learned much about working with the public from George, Marie, and Frances. In return, I was a fresh audience for their lifetime of stories. I was invited to dinners at their homes and included in Planetarium group events. Frances invited me to swim at Lanikai, and those beach days would turn into dinners with conversation. The many mementos around the house illustrated a life in Hawai`i and around the world and provoked questions, leading to storytelling around the monkeypod dining table.

As part of my internship, I was asked to do things like first, assist, and then solo, with Planetarium ticket taking. One of the challenges of getting visitors into the Planetarium shows was the late arriving ticket holder. The shows naturally require the room to be darkened. Once the patrons were seated, the lecturer would take the podium, start a general lead in and, using the control board, begin lowering the lights to let eyes adjust to the required total darkness. Patrons who arrived late needed to be taken into a vestibule between the outer and inner doors and held there while the outer door was closed. To ensure the inner darkness was preserved, the receptionist would turn on a flashlight equipped with a red filter to reduce the light, and then open the inner door. Guided by this flashlight, the late person was seated. One of Frances' great stories was about getting into the vestibule with a gentleman, only to find the flashlight didn't work. She told him, "I'm sorry, my batteries are dead." She would begin laughing as she repeated his reply, "That's okay, honey. My batteries died a long time ago."

My love for the Fraziers grew stronger with each passing year and we kept on seeing one another after their move to Kaua`i in 1976. I would visit and have adventures: Hal tried to teach me to drive a stick shift automobile in the upper pasture; the excitement of feeding over-ripe papaya to about a dozen cattle crowding the fence and more eager for the fruit than was safe for your hands.

Prepare to read some exciting tales and know, as I do, that Frances tells a great story: Weekends in Lanikai, lunches at the Planetarium basement, over the phone answering my questions about Hawai`i's "recent" history, I have been truly privileged to hear many of her stories. As a reader, you have the luck to be brought into her circle of listeners. Some stories share a pleasant memory (the hike across Mt. Ka'ala). Stories tell of meeting Hal while working at the Board of Water Supply. Stories recall anger (watching the December 7, 1941, attacks from the hills above Pearl Harbor–"we were being beaten and we weren't fighting back"). Stories recount what life was like in Hawai`i's war years (the soldier who wondered if Frances could "speak

English"). Stories express a frustration at not being able to change injustices (Pakistan remembrances) and taught me much about how blessed my life had really been. I count among the foremost blessings the wonderful fate that brought Frances and Hal into my life when I needed them most.

December, 2008
Waipahu, O'ahu, Hawai'i

About Anita Manning: *Born in Indiana and raised in San Diego, California, Anita is a 1969 graduate of San Diego State College. She came to Bernice Pauahi Bishop Museum from the San Diego Museum of Man in 1969 as one of five national recipients of a National Endowment for the Humanities grant. She spent twenty-six years with Bishop Museum, serving in Education, as Registrar, and finally as a Vice President–Assistant Director, and Corporate Secretary. She continues her association with the Museum as a volunteer Associate in Cultural Studies.*

Now self-employed as an historian and educator, Anita also works as husband Dr. Steven Montgomery's associate in biological consulting and applies her management skills to assist film makers working in Hawai'i. She is the author of articles on the history of science, Hawaiian history, and on museum management. She has traveled widely, from North America to Midway, Fanning Island, Guam, and the Marshall Islands.

~ ~ ~

Kathy Valier

My connection with Frances began through my father Louis Valier, who lectured part time at the Bishop Museum planetarium. Because of their friendship, I would often accompany my father during summer visits to Hanalei on his boat, "Tere," when he visited Hal and Frances after they moved to Kaua'i in 1976. I moved to Kaua'i in 1979, and they lived in an old-style board and batten house on the corner of Kahuna and Kawaihau Roads, a few miles inland from where my former husband and I built our house in Kapa'a.

Frances and I clicked because of our shared love for the outdoors and our down-to-earth, straightforward manner, and we began to get together even when my father was not on island. This led to her offering for me to ride her horse, Haukea; I only had to pay for his shoeing. Frances had hurt her back and so her days of riding her spirited Arabian gelding with her dear friend Jean Gregg, had come to an end. She and Jean had ridden many of the old cane roads through the abandoned fields behind Kapaʻa.

Haukea hated bridges and loved mangoes, as I soon learned in our rides down Kahuna Road. He would balk fearfully and very stubbornly and refuse to cross the old iron bridge there. It became a contest of our wills. When I finally induced him to cross, we passed under an old mango tree farther down the road where he again refused to budge, this time because he wanted to enjoy the mangoes that had fallen on the ground. He would stand there and endure my heels kicking at his ribs while he slurped the fruit up off the ground and ate, juice dripping from between his big lips. Then the seed would come popping out a minute later and he would be on to the next fruit.

One of my favorite stories not included in this memoir is about Frances riding Haukea through the recently abandoned pineapple fields in Wailua Homesteads, behind the Sleeping Giant. The plants were still producing ratoon pineapple and she stopped and picked one. Quite some time later they arrived home and after dismounting, Frances set the pineapple down for a moment while she loosened Haukea's saddle. In a flash, the horse snatched the pineapple and devoured it. "He must have been waiting the whole way back, thinking about that pineapple!" Frances said, laughing.

Frances and I both share a love for hiking, though her hiking days were over by the time she and Hal moved to Kauaʻi. The two hikes she talks about most were done when she was a member of the Piko Club on Oʻahu. This was during her time at the Board of Water Supply in Honolulu and before she and Hal married. She would accompany the Board's geologist, Chester Wentworth, on hikes all over Oʻahu. During that time she was invited to join the Piko (Summit) Club, which included mostly young Army officers. They would hike trails around Oʻahu, being dropped off and picked up at the far end–with refreshments–by military personnel.

One outstanding hike she did with the Piko Club was along the Koʻolau Summit trail. They began at the north shore and hiked some thirty-five miles by Frances' account, along the mountains behind Wahiawa. Another memorable trip she recounted to me was climbing 4,000-foot-tall Mount Ka'ala. Once on top, they crossed the flat, boggy summit where they stopped to have lunch with their feet dangling over the edge looking thousands of feet down onto the Wai'anae Coast.

The other part of Frances' life that intrigues me is the trip she took across the country with her father in 1936, after her high school graduation. She barely alludes to this trip in her memoir, but it must have been quite an adventure. I wish I'd had a tape recorder going when she described to me driving rough roads over the mountains into Mexico City. Her father's journal of this trip still exists and perhaps some day it can be shared too. I try to imagine what it was like for father and daughter to travel together and am reminded of hiking and sailing with my father and what rich times those were. And I wonder what it meant for her father to take his daughter back to his home to meet the woman for whom he had such a special place in his heart that he named his daughter after her.

In 1980s Hal and Frances moved from Kapa'a to 'Ōma'o. I house-sat for them and looked after their pets a couple of times when they went to stay at their cottage on Moloka'i. One other memory of Frances and Hal that stands out in my memory is visiting them at 'Ōma'o after Hurricane 'Iniki ripped the roof off their house. When we drove up all looked normal, because the roof was still intact on the south side of the house, but when we walked around the house, the entire north side of the structure was gone. Her beloved monkeypod table, at which we have enjoyed many meals, survived that storm. The only damage to it was a fine crack that developed along its length where two boards are joined.

Hal and Frances were living in their garage at the time and I remember driving away from that visit saying to my husband, "Two people in their eighties should not have to live like that." But as you read her account of that time in this memoir, Frances' true spirit shines through as she describes how she loved the simplicity and sense of community during that time. To her it was an adventure, not a hardship.

After my father passed away in 1995 and before my mother passed on in 2003, I would often spend the night when I was in town at Frances and Hal's Līhu'e Sun Village apartment, where they moved in latter years. I had been spending half of the year in New Zealand for seven years when my relationship there ended and I moved back to Kaua'i full time. Frances and I would walk with her little dog, Meali'il'i, around WalMart and be back at dawn. Stephanie was living on O'ahu at the time, my father was gone, and it just seemed natural to adopt each other, so I became her third *hānai* daughter. (Anita Manning and Noni Garner are the other "daughters" Frances informally adopted as adults.)

My thanks to Frances for sharing her stories, to Dawn Kawahara for her enthusiasm and persistence in bringing this project to completion, and to Anita Manning, another of Frances' *hānai*, for her support in this effort.

December, 2008
Wainiha, Kaua'i

About Kathy Valier: *Born in Honolulu in 1953, a handful of years after her parents wed and moved to Hawai'i, Kathy, like Frances, eschewed the social scene at school for the solitary joy of the ocean, in her case surfing. Her parents separated when she was ten and, as a result, she spent holidays exploring the islands with her father. Kathy received an undergraduate degree in English and Sociology at the University of Colorado in 1975. During those years she had the rare pleasure of sailing from Tahiti to Hawai'i with her father on his yacht, "Tere."*

After graduation, marriage, and the move to Kaua'i, she started a tour company, and later built a house with her husband. They sold the company and both returned to school on O'ahu, where she received a Master's Degree in Geography. She continued to guide groups through the islands on hiking and natural history tours. Her books, On The Nā Pali Coast *and* Ferns of Hawai'i *grew out of those experiences.*

Looking back, Kathy says, "I can see how our close relationships with seafaring fathers, love for hiking and the sea, and pragmatic, earthy approach to life led to the resonance between Frances and me."

~ ~ ~

MEMORIES of MOTHER

Stephanie Frazier

I am glad that Mom has so many daughters. I am the "real" daughter, Stephanie. My parents traveled away from me (or I from them) from 1963 to 1976. I learned to fend for myself and to grow up.

I went to join the Navy in Rhode Island in October, 1965, flunked out and went on to Washington, D.C., to live and work. I had jobs at the United States Department of Commerce and USAID (United States Agency for International Development) as a secretary. After two years there I moved to Albuquerque, New Mexico, to study Spanish at the University, thinking I would get a master's degree. I got married instead.

Mom said when she came to visit, "How can you live without the ocean nearby?" I said that the desert has wide expanses, plays of light on the landscape and beauty, as does the ocean. It is beautiful country. Also, New Mexico has a fascinating mix of cultures. I lived in Santa Fe and Albuquerque from about 1967 to 1976, when I returned to Hawai`i after my divorce.

About Mom's *hānai* daughters:

Noni Garner is the daughter of Vivian, Mom's dear friend. I remember childhood adventures with them. I often went to their home in Manoa Valley in early years. I got to know Sanford Zalburg, Noni's step dad, better in later years, after Vivian died in 1981. Noni moved to the Bay Area in the late 1970's, I believe, and I talk with her by phone and see her on occasional visits.

I first met Kathy Valier in 1976 or so when I left the Mainland and returned to Kaua`i to visit my folks. I moved on to O`ahu and then returned to Kaua`i in October, 2000, when I got tired of O`ahu's "rat race." I have gotten to know her better since, and I am so grateful for her regular visits and additional help to Mom.

I knew Anita Manning in the early 1980's when I visited her and husband Steve near the Ala Wai canal in Honolulu, where they had an apartment. I have talked to her on the phone, mostly about

Mom's welfare. I did not know she was informally "adopted" until a few years ago.

There is another woman, Deborah Byrnes, whom I would like to mention. She has become a close helper and friend to Mom and Dad starting in 2004, when Mom needed help with driving, cooking, and companionship.

Noni was always in our family group. I first learned that Mom had "adopted" Anita as they worked together and she would visit Mom and Dad on Kaua`i and go with them to Koke`e and other favorite places. Kathy was "adopted" in the 1970's, as I mentioned.

My mom has always been supportive of me. I remember as a child she taught me to cook and to clean. We had a home on acreage that looked down into a jungle leading to Nu`uanu Stream. My brother and I and friends played there. We always had pets. I often rode horses with Mom at Kapi`olani Park. I spent my teen years doing that, along with studying. I was assigned to household chores and my brother, to outside chores. Dad helped me to get a scholarship to Punahou where I got a great education. Mom and Vivian encouraged me to find my way, which was difficult at times. My parents often traveled due to Dad's job as an engineer. They left me in the hands of caregivers, including a couple from Ni`ihau who were studying education at university.

I was not aware that Mom was a journalizer, like her father, my Grandfather Nelson, until recent years. In Pakistan she had time on her hands, not being able to go freely about on the streets. After her return, I noted her to be very busy translating the deeds and other documents. I don't know how she found the time to journalize at home.

October, 2009
Lihu`e, Kaua`i, Hawai`i

About Stephanie Frazier: After returning to her home state, Stephanie worked for many years as a medical transcriptionist. She currently works as a voice recognition editor of medical reports.

ACKNOWLEDGMENTS

Sincere thanks go to all who have contributed in various supportive ways to this book in its preparation of manuscript, graphics and book design on Kaua`i by Dawn F. Kawahara, TropicBird Press, Wailua, Hawai`i. (See Preface: Editor's Notes of thanks.)

Additionally,

Book formatting, printing, binding and other related services: AuthorHouse Services, Bloomington, Indiana.

Cover photograph: Dana Edmunds Photography, Kailua, O`ahu, Hawai`i.

Letters and papers of Frances N. Frazier, and archival photos and documents: Frances N. Frazier Trust, Stephanie Frazier, Trustee.

Maps: Courtesy of the University Libraries, The University of Texas at Austin.

"Tillie E. Starbuck" photograph: courtesy Purdue University Library, West Lafayette, IN: Donald H. Dyal Ship Collection (Nautical Photo Agency, 1849).

"St. Mary's" photograph: Department of the Navy, Naval Historical Center (CUP), Washington Navy Yard, DC.

All other photographs: per accompanying photo credits.

`*ekahi* / one

BEGINNINGS

1914 to 1950s

GENEALOGY

The information given in the following genealogy charts (A and B) has been taken directly from the author's telling in the chapters of this book, her papers and documents. It is a Hawaiian tradition to begin any formal cultural presentation with a recitation of genealogy, as in the *Kumulipo* (Hawaiian genesis chant [Beckwith 1951 and Johnson 1981]). Note the form used stressing the maternal line, also traditional, since Hawaiian blood lines were traced matrilineally, or with emphasis on the Mother, right back to the mythological genealogy of the volcano goddess Pele.

The reason for chanting genealogy in the oral tradition–or preserving it on paper–is to document from which roots the generational leaves and branches grow. The charts of personal information of a native daughter of Hawai'i and her Hawai'i-born husband may prove interesting to the reader because of the many "voyagers" who sailed from far and distant places and eventually pooled bloodlines (not only in Hawai'i, but in the New World–and all around the globe). An aside: As known scientifically today, this infusion of genes strengthens the DNA of original settlers.– **Ed.**

(Beginning [as known]
AUTHOR'S MATERNAL
Line – **CHART A***)*

(Beginning [as known]
AUTHOR'S
PATERNAL Line)

Hendryka van Vliet
(Dutchwoman of New
Amsterdam)
m. 164_(?) John Nelson
(English, emigrated
to America 1640)

✳

Great-grandmother:
Keokilele
b. 1827 (Wainiha, Kaua`i)
m. Oct. 20, 1855
(Wai`oli, Kaua`i)
Great-grandfather:
G. W. Coggeshall
div. 1873 (Coggeshall
deserted Mar. 23, 1870,
"sailed to another
country," leaving 9
living [of 10] children)

✳

[some generations later]
Great-grandmother:
(Name/birthdate
unknown)
m. descendant of van
Vliet-Nelson forebears,
Great-grandfather:
Elisha Nelson (Land
owner "highlands of
the Hudson," New
York (NY) [hamlet of
Nelsonville])

✳

Grandmother:
Sarah Coggeshall Cook
b. Aug. 27, 1858
(adopted 1870s
by Thomas Cook,
Surveyor of Hilo)
m. 1876 (Kealakekua,
S. Kona, Hawai`i)
Grandfather:
William Todd
(Saddlemaker, Hilo Fire
Chief), b. Oct. 1, 1856

✳

Grandmother:
Martha "Mattie" Jane
Nelson (Homemaker)
b. Mar. 10, 1848 (NY)
m. 1873
Grandfather:
Julian Tracy Smith
(Clockwords maker,
Purchasing Agent,
Scoville Mfg., Waterbury,
Connecticut), b. Nov.
12, 1844, d. Oct. 3, 1931

✳

Mother:
Ellen Eva Todd
(Telephone operator–one
of the first in Hilo)
b. June 10, 1880
(Hilo, Hawai`i)
d. Jan. 14, 1956

↔

m. Dec. 8, 1902
(Hilo, Hawai`i)

↕

Father:
Richard Nelson Smith
(Master Mariner,
Ships' Captain)
[Dropped "Smith," took
mother's maiden name
"Nelson" in his teens]
b. Aug 22, 1876
(Ocean Beach [now
Delmar] New Jersey)
d. Feb. 11, 1960

Frances Nelson
(Translator, Hawaiian
Language)
b. July 6, 1914
(Honolulu, O`ahu)
m. Feb. 26, 1938
Harold Victor Frazier
(Civil Engineer), b. July
29, 1911 (Honolulu,
O`ahu), d. Mar. 15, 2004
(Līhu`e, Kaua`i, HI)

↕

CHILDREN

✳

Douglas Frazier
b. Nov. 29, 1939
(Honolulu, O`ahu, HI)
m. Diane Moore
d. Dec. 2, 1981

↔

✳

Stephanie Frazier
b. Oct. 17, 1942
(Honolulu, O`ahu, HI)
m./div.

↕

GRANDCHILDREN

Cheryl Frazier (m.
Dwayne Kuilipule)
Lisa Leinaala Frazier
[of "Letter to Lisa"] (m./
div. Tyson Jardine)
Kristin Mahealani
Frazier

↵

✳   ✳   ✳

*(Beginning [as known]
AUTHOR'S Husband's
MATERNAL Line –
CHART B*)*

*(Beginning [as known]
AUTHOR'S Husband's
PATERNAL Line)*

Grandmother:
Marie Schultz (Polish-
German extraction,
emigrated from Berlin,
Germany, 1858;
Housemaid and
homemaker,
Chicago, Illinois)
m. 18_(?)_

Grandfather:
(Name unknown)
Parsyczk (emigrated
from Poland, 1856;
Lumber worker,
union organizer,
Assistant, Samuel
Gompers, American
Federation of Labor)

✻

✻

Mother:
Marie Parsyczk
b. 1878

↔

m. 1911 (Chicago,
Illinois, U.S.A.)

↕

Father:
Charles Franklin
Frazier, b. 1882
(Contractor; Colonel,
U.S. Army)

Harold Victor
Frazier (Engineer)
b. July 29, 1911
(Honolulu, Oʻahu)
m. Frances Ellen Nelson
(Honolulu, Oʻahu)
d. Mar. 15, 2004
(Līhuʻe, Kauaʻi, HI)

[Children and grandchildren
as shown in Chart A]

LETTER to LISA

April 7, Easter Sunday, 1996

Dear Lisa,

Thank you for your Easter card and letter. Happy Easter to you and yours, too.

This may be the best of times and yet the worst of times to tell you that I have been on a spiritual journey which has not recognized any particular religious organization as being important to me. I do feel that there is a power which rules the universe but have always wondered whether we humans are capable of recognizing it.

Your letter with all those questions aroused so many recollections that I would have to write a book to answer them all. I am afraid your grandfather and I have not been very good models as grandparents. We have been separated by distance and the various jobs we have held. But even though we haven't been able to see you very often, we care about you all and I will try to share with you the information I have collected so that you and your sisters will have some knowledge of your family history, or perhaps I should say histories.

You have called me *Tūtū* and your grandfather *Tūtū Kāne*, and that is good, since it commemorates the fact that through me you have inherited a small amount of Hawaiian blood, which is mixed with a rainbow of other racial mixtures. You should never forget those drops of Hawaiian blood because through them you are connected to the ancient past of this archipelago.

I will try to arrange a sequence of events which led up to the appearance of yourself and your sisters into the world. But I must warn you that I might get caught up in my reminiscences. Our Hawaiian ancestors had a saying: `O ke ola he alanui kīke`eke`e, "Life is a road with many turns."

I was born in Honolulu when it was a nice little town, and every boat day was lei-day. There were no airplanes bringing new faces and ideas to Hawai'i *nei* when I arrived on the scene. There were no high-rise buildings and little Waikīkī was a dreamy spot to go swimming and surfing, with only the Moana Hotel standing on the beach–this, the first step by developers who eventually made the place unrecognizable to me.

At the time of my birth my parents were living on the slopes of Punchbowl, a small volcanic crater whose slopes rose abruptly back of the town. Punchbowl is now the site of a National Cemetery for the war dead.

As this story meanders on you will learn a lot more about me, but I think we'll start with *Tūtū Kāne* because without him there wouldn't have been any of you.

His full name is Harold Victor Frazier, Hal for short, and his parents were Charles Franklin Frazier (called Frank) and Marie Jean Parsyczk Frazier. It is not known exactly where the Fraziers came from and how they ended up in a little town in West Virginia called Newberg.

The name Frazier is probably French, because of its spelling, although in that little area in West Virginia there are many people of Scottish-Irish descent and the name could be Scottish.

In Virginia there is a little town called Frazier's Corners and Great-grandfather Frazier had a farm in the vicinity. An attempt has been made to link the name to the French, through the word *fraises,* strawberries. One particular legend ties in with a story that two French soldiers left Quebec after the defeat of the French, and started walking south until they got to Virginia or West Virginia.

The main line of the Baltimore and Ohio Railway runs through Newberg, and Harold's grandfather was a locomotive engineer. In those days, of course, grandmas stayed home and raised families so we don't have much information on his grandmother. Harold remembers as a child helping his grandma make apple butter in a big iron kettle out in the yard once when he was visiting them.

Harold's father Frank Frazier, born in 1882, had a grade school education and then was put to work for a contractor in railway tunnels which were being enlarged. In 1903 he enlisted in the Army and served in it until he finally retired in 1946 as a Colonel.

Frank Frazier's wife, born in 1878 and named Marie Parsyczk, was of Polish-German blood. Marie's father was a blacksmith who emigrated from Poland in 1856 and settled first in Chicago and then in Marinette, Wisconsin, which in those days was a lumbering town. He married a German woman named Marie Schultz, who emigrated from Berlin in 1858 and worked as a housemaid in Chicago. He worked for the lumber company until he was badly injured after which he returned to Chicago and became an assistant to Samuel Gompers, who founded the American Federation of Labor (AFL). Because of the neglect by his former employers who did not assist him when he was injured, he proceeded to organize and unionize the entire lumber operation in Wisconsin.

Frank Frazier and Marie Parsyczk met and were married in 1911 in Chicago, where Frank was on the Army rifle team competing in that area. From Chicago they went briefly to Fort Leavenworth, Kansas, the home base of the Third Army Engineers, and from there they went directly to Hawai`i where his regiment was engaged in building Fort Shafter, Fort Kamehameha, and Fort Ruger on the island of O`ahu.

During that period they lived in tents, moving from area to area. Harold was born in Honolulu on July 29, 1911, at the old Kapi`olani Maternity Hospital. So he really is a *keiki o ka `āina,* child of the land. They returned to the United States Mainland at the beginning of World War I. While serving abroad, Frank was gassed by the Germans, and after a term in Arizona as an invalid, he became the military instructor at California Institute of Technology. In 1921 he returned to Hawai`i to Schofield Barracks.

As is typical in the army, Harold's parents moved periodically on different assignments and his education was: "Born in Hawai`i, educated in Brooklyn, etc. etc." He attended three years at the University of Hawai`i at Manoa, and then when his father was stationed at the Presidio in San Francisco, he attended the University of California at Berkeley and was graduated as a civil engineer in 1935.

After graduation Harold came back to Hawai`i from San Francisco and worked for the Hawaiian Sugar Planters Association, then for the Board of Water Supply in Honolulu, where we met. I was at that time working as a stenographer at the Engineering Office of the Board of Water Supply.

The Engineering Office had actually been the City and County of Honolulu's mule stable. It stood right next door to the Beretania Pumping Station. I was the only female in the engineering office. My work was typing reams of specifications and engineering reports and also geological reports written by Chester K. Wentworth, the geologist who worked for the Board of Water Supply. I also took care of the phone calls.

I still remember my first sight of Hal: a very, very tall young man with a straw hat, standing at the entrance to the Engineering Office. He had been hired to work on one of the tunnel jobs then being done by the Board of Water Supply.

In 1936 my father and I embarked from Honolulu on the ship "Matsonia" to begin a four-month journey around the United States, Mexico and part of Canada, ending up at the little village of Cold Spring, New York, on the Hudson River, across and a bit upstream from West Point. My father wanted me to see his ancestral home. It happened that Harold was on board too, going to visit his parents at the Presidio in San Francisco, and while on board a very long and (mostly) happy marriage had its beginnings in a little spark of electricity that passed between us on this voyage.

We were married on February 26, 1938, in Honolulu. I continued to work at the Board of Water Supply until the arrival of our son Douglas–who grew up to become your father–was imminent.

When I am finished with this *mo'olelo* (which means story), you will have a pretty good idea of what the blood in your veins is composed of. There are so many strands woven into it.

Once upon a time I had an altercation with a Japanese man. This was just after the end of World War II. He was our neighbor on 'Aiea Heights where Harold and I lived, in a shack, when we were first married. This man was embittered because he had been confined in a concentration camp throughout World War II because of his undoubted sympathies with Japan. His final words to me were, "You are nothing but a mongrel, whereas I (thumping his chest), am a pure Japanese!" It didn't bother me because I am comfortable in my own skin.

We in our family are not pure anything–we are a grand and glorious mixture and when you get through reading our story, think about your mom's parents and their parents and how that is all stirred into the mixture that is you. Every once in a while some particular gene seems to predominate and a family likeness will pop up. For instance, when your Aunt Stephanie was born she was the image of your Great-grandmother Marie Parsyczk. Later the resemblance faded, but it was striking when she was an absolutely "tow-haired" baby.

Your father Douglas "took" on my side–he had my coloring. I remember once in a service station with the two children visible in the car a facetious worker remarked in classic Pidgin, "E, how come, one light, one dark?"

As regards myself: On the paternal side, my information goes back to the year 1640 when an Englishman named John Nelson arrived in New Amsterdam, where he met and married a Dutch girl named Hendryka van Vliet. The next bit of information is that an Elisha Nelson, descended from John, had taken up quite a lot of land in what is sometimes called the Highlands of the Hudson, with Storm King Mountain just across the river. This is Rip Van Winkle country.

There is still a little hamlet called Nelsonville, named after my ancestor, just above the village of Cold Spring which is where my grandmother's people lived. The summer I visited there and stayed with Great-aunt Nina, there would be a rolling sound of thunder every afternoon. Aunt Nina would quietly excuse herself and descend into the basement kitchen of the pre-Revolutionary house which had housed many Nelsons. There she would wait out the thunderstorm, for, as she explained to me, she had been afraid of the sound of thunder her whole life. (Fortunately for me, when I was a child and frightened of thunder and lightning, my father would take me out on the veranda to watch and admire the drama.)

Elisha Nelson was my great-grandfather. He was extremely religious according to information I got from the Putnam County Historical Society, and from my father. His daughter Mattie Nelson married Julian Tracy Smith and had my father, Richard Nelson Smith and his brother Tracy Smith. I remember that Mattie and Julian Smith came and lived with us in Honolulu when Grandfather Julian became unable to endure the winters in New England. He died in

Honolulu and Mattie went back to Cold Spring to live with her sister, Nina Nelson Newman. I believe that life in Hawai`i was rather a shock to my New England Grandmother–things were a bit too loose and easy in Hawai`i for someone of her strict upbringing.

I know nothing at all about my Grandfather Julian Tracy Smith, except that all his life he worked in Waterbury, Connecticut, for the Scovill Manufacturing Company, which I believe made things like precision clocks, and probably other types of machinery. He was, like my grandmother, a strict and upright man, and a very handsome man, as I remember.

My father Richard Nelson Smith, born August 22, 1876, was a non-conformist from the very beginning, I imagine. He told me once that he rebelled against the constant religious atmosphere in his home and as a reaction he became an atheist. When my *haole* ("foreign," usually implying Caucasian) grandparents lived with us in Honolulu he would drive them every Sunday to the Central Union Church and wait for them in the car while they went to church service and my older brother Dick and I went to Sunday School. I don't remember that my mother went to church with them.

Actually it must have been quite a shock to my *haole* grandparents to realize that their son had married a Hawaiian woman. I remember the stricken look on my grandmother's face when my older brother Dick married Pearl Harbottle, who was even more Hawaiian than my mother.

I am getting ahead a bit. . .

FATHER'S SEA LIFE, MOTHER'S MOTHER

Since my father did not fit in at home, he went to New York to live with a Nelson uncle and aunt. They made him their ward and since he wanted to go to sea, they arranged for him to take the name of Nelson. As a resident of New York City he was eligible to go on the New York City training vessel called "St. Mary," for young men who wanted to become seafarers. Once aboard, they were taught the arts of sailing, including navigation.

It must have been a rigorous life on board. My father kept a diary and in later life he wrote it up as a history of his travels.[1] There are some amazingly good photographs he took on shipboard with a little box camera, way back then. I made a copy of the journal and gave the original with its photographs to the Hawai`i State Archives. He told me once that all the cadets had to run up one side of the rigging and down the other side before breakfast.

At the end of his time on the "St. Mary" he was offered the opportunity to go to Annapolis and become a Navy officer, but again, being a non-conformist, he refused the opportunity and instead shipped on the "Tillie Starbuck," which he told me was the first sailing vessel made with an iron hull (not steel) instead of a wooden hull.

Making the passage around Cape Horn–this was before the Panama Canal was built–was the only way to get to the Pacific from the East Coast (unless you went all the other way around). He told me once that no one on board ever had any dry clothes or blankets during the time it took to beat their way against terrible storms to get to the Pacific Ocean. It surely was the test of what made a man. Once they had the experience of being dismasted off Cape Hatteras, so they had to go back and get re-rigged and then make another attempt to get past Hatteras, which had a bad reputation but not as bad as Cape Horn.

The best book I ever read on the subject of sail was *Two Years Before the Mast* by Richard Dana. Father had a copy in our library and I read it over again recently. I was charmed by Dana's descriptions of his friendship with some Hawaiians who were stranded in California

13

and living on the beach. He must have had a good ear for language because when I re-read his book (with my present knowledge of Hawaiian), I could not find any errors in the Hawaiian phrases he recorded.

I recently learned that a direct descendant of Richard Dana lives right here on Kaua'i. His name is Ned Dana and I met him through computers. One day when we happened to sit next each other on a flight to Honolulu, I told him how much I liked *Two Years Before the Mast*, and asked him if by any chance he could be a descendant of Richard Dana. He smiled and said that Richard Dana was his great-grandfather, and also told me that his other great-grandfather was Henry Wadsworth Longfellow!

My father hated cold weather, and he told me once he was caught coming home from school in a particularly grim blizzard in the 1860s. Luckily he made it to a house where a kind woman warmed him up with a cup of hot chocolate. The winters in that part of the country got so cold that the Hudson River would freeze over. My Great-aunt Nina told me that when she was a girl they would skate over to the other side of the river.

Father made a number of trips in the "Tillie Starbuck." Finally he left the ship and went ashore at Honolulu in 1897. He went to work for the Wilder Steamship Company and then the Inter-Island Steam Navigation Company, finally becoming a captain of some of their ships. He left the steamship company in 1913 to become a harbor pilot in Pearl Harbor.

Those little steamships visited all the ports in the Hawaiian archipelago and where there were no ports, they used a "wire landing." They would anchor offshore below the cliffs, wherever there was a little town or a sugar plantation. There they used a wire landing, which consisted of a cable, winch and pulleys, run from the top of the cliff down to a block of concrete where it would be secured until a ship came. Then the cable would be taken out to the ship and the cargo, passed up or down the cable. Many tons of sugar were loaded in that way, plus supplies for the little settlement.

My father met my mother, Ellen Eva Todd, born on June 10, 1880, in Hilo.

My mother's mother was Sarah Coggeshall Cook Todd, whom I remember with affection after all these long years, even though she lived in Hilo and I seldom saw her. But our meetings were memorable. In fact, since I had never been given a Hawaiian name, I took for myself the name *Hali'a-aloha-no-ke-kupuna* which means "fond recollection of the grandparent." So now I am known by my Hawaiian friends as Hali`a, meaning "fond recollection."

Whenever she came to Honolulu to visit us, my Grandmother Todd would stop off first on Maui to visit friends and relatives, and when she got to our house she always had a bottle of "Maui corn" whiskey with her. She used to invite me into her room, look at me and say: "You're too *wīwī* (skinny)," and she would administer me a tiny shot of her whiskey, much to Mother's disapproval. I can't blame mother for disapproving because she was so ashamed of her father's being such a drunkard. But I guess Grandmother Sarah took her husband's carousing in stride or she would have had the same prejudice against alcohol that my mother had. Mother told me that she was so shamed by her father's drinking that she joined the Salvation Army and sang in the streets of Hilo, and as a result he reformed.

Because my Grandmother Sarah had always lived in Hilo and my mother was born there, I thought Sarah was born on the island of Hawai`i. But I discovered that she was actually born Sarah Coggeshall on the island of Kaua`i, and that her ancestors had lived at Wainiha on Kaua`i. Sarah's mother was named Keokilele and had been married to a man named G. W. Coggeshall by whom she had nine surviving children.

In 1974 when I was working as Hawaiian Translator at the Hawai`i State Archives, I had occasion to go upstairs to the vault. While I was looking for a folder in a particular file cabinet, I saw the name Keokilele on a folder, which I knew was my great-grandmother's name. So I took it out and read it, and it explained why my grandmother had lived in Hilo.

I recognize and am grateful for this and other coincidences that have occurred in my life a number of times. Once in a while we are given glimpses of a pathway on which we are seemingly guided from childhood, and happy is the person who is able to follow the

15

pathway that is offered, because those are the people who can accept themselves as they are.

The letter was all in Hawaiian and it was written by Keokilele to Judge Hardy, asking for a divorce from Coggeshall. She stated that she had been married to G. W. Coggeshall at Hanalei, by the first Hawaiian minister to serve at Wai'oli, on October 20, 1855. They were married for fifteen years and had ten children, nine of whom were living. She said that on March 23, 1870, her husband left her and the children and "sailed to another country" and she "had no further knowledge of his whereabouts." Therefore, she stated, she and the children were destitute.

She was granted a divorce. Later, she married John Malina of Kipu, Kaua'i, and had eight more children.

My Grandmother Sarah was the second child of Keokilele's nine surviving children with Coggeshall, born August 27, 1858. Since Keokilele was destitute after Coggeshall's departure, Sarah was adopted by a man I believe to have been a friend of Coggeshall's named Thomas Cook, a surveyor, and taken to Hilo, where she lived the rest of her life.

Sarah Coggeshall married William Todd at Kealakekua, South Kona, Hawai'i, in 1876. They lived in Hilo all their lives and Sarah bore twelve children. My mother Ellen was the second of the children. William Todd's father, my great-grandfather, was an Englishman who had come early to Hawai'i and had become a naturalized subject of the Hawaiian Kingdom, and had married a woman named Ellen Woods. I have never been able to trace my Great-grandmother Ellen's background and racial mixture although, like my mother, I bore her name (my given middle maiden name–Frances Ellen Nelson). Since in those early years men came to Hawai'i and woman rarely did (except for missionary wives), it is likely that Great-grandmother Ellen had some Hawaiian blood, which would make my Grandfather William part-Hawaiian. Certainly, my mother looked at least half-Hawaiian.

My Todd great-grandparents had a small boarding house or hotel in Kona, on the Island of Hawai'i, above a place named Captain Cook. In *Six Months in the Sandwich Islands*, a fascinating account of early Hawai'i written by a very adventurous Englishwoman, Isabella

L. Bird Bishop, mention is made of my great-grandparents and of her stay at their establishment.

Grandfather Todd was a famous saddle-maker and leather worker whose saddles were much in demand. He was the fire chief in Hilo for a number of years, and later was a Supervisor in Hilo County for some years. He was also a famous drunk; his Saturday night celebrations with Marcus Monsarrat were the talk of Hilo. My mother, who was one of the very first telephone operators in Hilo after such a new-fangled thing came to town, was determined to shame her father into stopping so, as I mentioned earlier, she joined the Salvation Army and sang in the streets of Hilo. It worked.

While at the Archives I came across Grandfather Todd's obituary published in Hawaiian, which I translated and keep in my genealogical files. I was tickled by the mention of his nickname in the obituary. He was called "Huro," which means *Hurrah!* I imagine it referred to his high-spirited days with John Barleycorn.

My mother Ellen met my father Richard Nelson in Hilo, and they were married on December 8, 1902. They had three children: Richard II, myself (Frances), and Julian. My father was at that time employed by the Inter-Island Steam Navigation Company, which owned both small, passenger steamers and freighters, which served all the Hawaiian Islands.

He served as captain of several Inter-Island ships. As a Master Mariner he was sent to the Mainland a couple of times to bring back a new ship for the steamship line.

I was born on July 6, 1914, in Honolulu and was the second child. My older brother Dick was born in 1912, and my younger brother Julian was born in 1918. I believe my parents were living at Watertown, at Pearl Harbor, when I was born because I have a babyhood recollection of being in my mother's arms on a launch in Pearl Harbor, where some sort of celebration was taking place.

My younger brother Julian worked for the Hawaiian Pineapple Company his whole working career, in the cannery. He married Evelyn Yap, whose father and mother operated a little store right at the corner of Kamāmalu Avenue and `Iolani Avenue. As children we used to go into the store and purchase *see moi* ("crackseed"), and

17

dried abalone, and other Chinese goodies. Mr. Yap was rather a dour person as I remember, but the rest of the family was very jolly.

Julian and Evelyn had two sons–Billie, who now lives in California, and Allan, who lives near his mother in Hawai`i Kai on the island of O`ahu.

Because of our wandering life, in later years we have missed being in close contact with my nephews and their children. Julian died a couple of years ago; Evelyn invited me to go out in the boat when Julian's ashes were deposited in the ocean, out where the ashes of our father and mother already were scattered.

I am approaching my ninetieth birthday as I write this, and all this took place so very long ago.

EARLY YEARS

The home where I grew up was at 1619 Kamāmalu Avenue, on the slope of Punchbowl overlooking Honolulu Harbor. My father had gotten the job of harbor pilot at Honolulu Harbor. From our house he was able to walk down to the harbor, which he preferred to do rather than drive our car. Being a seafaring man, he liked to be able to see the harbor and the ocean. Now tall buildings block the view of the harbor.

In those days there was no radio contact with ships; there was a watchman stationed out on Diamond Head. He had a little house just past the Diamond Head Lighthouse. There was a big bay window with a large telescope in it. As soon as Mr. Brown, the watchman, spotted a ship, he would telephone the pilots' office at Honolulu for the pilot who was on duty. There would be just time enough for my father to walk down to the waterfront and board the pilot launch and go out to meet the ship. He would have to climb up the "Jacob's ladder" to get on board.

Mr. Brown and my father were friends. Father, who did not smoke (or drink alcohol), would take him a present of a box of cigars, which it was customary for ship captains to present to the pilots as a gift. The captains would also give fine French cognac, or good Scotch whiskey, which my father brought home under his coat (because it was during the time of Prohibition), and the only time such liquors were consumed was when Mother made her annual Christmas fruitcakes, and she would put a jigger or so into the batter.

My great childhood pleasure was to go down to the waterfront with my father and board the pilot launch with him. I would sit up in the bow while we went out to meet the ship, and watch my father climb up the "Jacob's ladder," which was dangerous on stormy days. then the launch would return to port and the boat-boy, as I called him, would drop me off at the Pilots' Office on Pier 7, where I would wait for my father to return.

This went on for a few years until one day, when I had entered my early teens, my father looked me over and said, "You're getting too big to be hanging around the waterfront." So that was the end of a time I had found enjoyable.

My older brother and I played with the children across the street, mostly the Aluli family. They had a Hawaiian maid who lived with them in a little basement apartment. Her family was named Kaniaupio, and they owned *kuleana* land up in Maunawili Valley, which is over on the Kailua side of Nu'uanu Pali–the windward side of O'ahu. Lily and I became fast friends and I spent a lot of time with her, although she was at least fifteen years older. She informally adopted me, as Hawaiians do. I can call up her face now, with affection.

Our family used to go camping at Kualoa, on the beach not far from the ruins of the old sugar mill, which had a tragic story attached to it. It seems that one of the little boys in the Judd family was walking a plank laid across a vat of boiling molasses, and he fell in and was killed, after which the mill was abandoned. My recollections of this story might be a little off, but I don't think so. We used to sleep in hammocks which were slung from the branches of the *kamani* (Indian almond) trees which grew all along that particular stretch of beach. Nowadays it is all built up with homes and our camp site is only a memory.

In 1924, when I was about ten years old, my parents bought a couple of lots right on the beach in Ka'ohao. This is the real name of the ancient little land division tucked in between Kailua and Waimānalo. It was actually an '*ili* (Hawaiian land division) named Ka'ohao. The developers named the place Lanikai, and divided it into house lots.

Lanikai is cut off from the other districts by a curved line of hills on the inland side and by the sea on the other side. According to the Pukui, Elbert and Mookini *Place Names of Hawai'i*, one of the meanings of Ka'ōhao is "to tie" or "the tying," and I always envisioned it as the knot which held Kailua and Waimānalo together. The shoreline faced a little north of east, and on very clear days Moloka'i island could be seen, with a white line of beach. The solstice point was between the two islands named Mokulua (which means "Two Islands"), and I remember spectacular sunrises there. Sometimes I would go out with my older brother and a couple of friends to the larger of the two islands named Mokulua. It has a fascinating crevice which runs right through the island, from one side to the other, supported by great basalt dikes, and the ocean can be heard booming inside the island.

I spent every weekend and all summer long during all my growing up years at Lanikai with my mother and brothers. My father would join us when he was not on standby duty as a pilot. In 1924, our tiny house was the only one at that end of Lanikai–I used to have a photograph taken from the hill looking down over Lanikai, and there was our one little house, standing all alone.

I was alone most of the time because mother was always at her quilt frame and my older brother was off with his friends. Being solitary by nature, I found great pleasure in walking on the long beach in the early mornings, and in swimming or sailing on the reef-protected waters. In later years, I realized that in my pre-teen and teen years I probably missed out on a lot of social contacts with young people my own age, but I never ever regretted it because my wonderful, free childhood in Lanikai was enough to keep me happy. I had a pony to ride sometimes, and I would ride around the point into Waimānalo, or over the other way to Kailua.

Later on I had a little Moth sailboat which was great fun to sail because, for the size of its hull, it had a tremendous mast and sail. It was really fast, but it was also very tetchy and you could capsize if you weren't alert every moment. My brother got a motorboat and father built us an "aquaplane," which was the forerunner of waterskis. It was simply a board with a rope bridle, towed by our motorboat. You held on and balanced with the rope bridle. Lots of fun. You had to be careful, as you are with a surfboard, not to get too far forward or you would be in trouble.

I have mused, as I grow older, about the things I saw which will never be seen again. For instance, the enormous flights of `iwa, the frigate bird. In the luminous hours just before sunrise, I would watch hundreds and hundreds of these birds, floating on an air current high in the sky overhead. They were all moving towards the northeast, perhaps going home to their nests after a night of piracy, or, on the other hand, perhaps setting out for a day of pillage. I did not know which, but I was a silent witness of their passage.

Sometimes mother's best friend Lena Cunningham and her three children, Madalyn, Trancita and Jimmy would come for the weekend. Lily Kaniaupio would sometimes come to visit us at Lanikai. I would go with her to pick *limu* off the rocks at the point between Lanikai and Waimānalo. Or she would take me home with her to Maunawili and I would spend time with her and her family. They had enormous *pua kenikeni* trees in their yard, and Lily made me many a fragrant lei.

This Hawaiian family was living in the old way, growing their own taro, living on fish and *poi,* I cherish my memories of them all. When Lily's mother died she was buried in their garden and I attended the services. There, for the first time I heard the *uwē*, the mourning chants of the family, and it was an unforgettable experience.

When I look about the apartment which we have chosen to be our final domicile, there are a number of objects which I have inherited from my *haole* ancestors, which I have preserved through various moves and travels because they have memories for me and because they are beautiful. There are Oriental rugs on the floor which were collected during my travels, as well as those which I inherited from my *haole* grandparents.

However, there are no artifacts from the Hawaiian side of my family, save for a stone *poi* pounder which serves as a door-stop.

Getting to Lanikai was an adventure in those early 1920s. The first adventure was getting around the windy corner where the Nu`uanu Pali road began to descend into Kane`ohe. It was a common occurrence for touring cars with canvas tops to lose their tops on especially windy days. We always had to be sure things were well secured or they would blow right out of the car.

Once I lost a brand-new pair of silk pajamas which had been thrown carelessly on the back seat. There was no tunnel at that time, just the turn around the corner and down the narrow road that wound down to Kane`ohe and Kailua. In the rainy months there were often landslides which blocked the road. Then, even though we might have negotiated the Pali Road successfully, on a rainy, muddy day it might not be possible to get up the steep incline which led up to where Castle Memorial Hospital now stands. Then we'd have to turn around and go back to Honolulu.

School for me began at a dame school (a school taught by young, unmarried women teachers), called the Valley School, which was right at the intersection of Pauoa Road and Nu`uanu Avenue. All the classes of young children were taught in one room. The older ones were taught in a separate room. I used to walk there from 1619 Kamāmalu Avenue, all by myself, and home again, starting at the age of six. In those long-ago days my parents never thought a thing about sending a little one like me to school all alone. How times have changed!

At the second grade I was transferred to Central Grammar School on Emma Street, which was a much shorter distance for me to walk. The property on which Central Grammar School stood had formerly belonged to Princess Ruth Ke'elikolani. The mansion called Keōuahale, which Princess Ruth had built, was the centerpiece of the school campus and was where the administration offices were. I remember my arithmetic teacher's face to this day. I am sure I was a sore trial to her because of my ineptitude with numbers. Anyway, whether it was all my fault or not, she was a sourpuss.

Then the Department of Education started a controversial "English standard" school called Lincoln School on Beretania Street right across from Thomas Square. This was for children who spoke an acceptable kind of English (not Pidgin). I have always had trouble with fractions and have often wondered whether the fact that I skipped a grade when I transferred to that school was the reason I have always had problems with the subject. Probably not. I simply was not gifted in mathematics. On the other hand, English grammar was easy and words and their derivation have always fascinated me.

When I graduated from Lincoln School in the eighth grade, my parents asked me if I wanted to go to Punahou, the private high school known for its high standard of education. I chose to go to McKinley High School instead.

At this time of my life it became apparent to me that there was no love between my father and mother, only tolerance, and I decided to make my own way in the world and depend on myself to find my own security.

However they felt about each other, their ashes are resting together in the sea between Mokulua–the two islands just offshore of Lanikai. They both loved our place on the beach at Lanikai, from which you could look straight out to the two islands. They both requested that this be done and we, the children, saw to it when my mother, and later my father, died. There were no ceremonies, which was also as they requested.

When I graduated from McKinley High School, I elected to go to Miss Tabitha Phillips' business school, located in an old Victorian style house on Makiki Heights. I attended for about a year, until I was sent as a temporary worker to the Board of Water Supply. The temporary job became permanent, and I stayed with the Board of Water Supply for a total of nine years.

MARRIED LIFE BEGINS

One day (as mentioned before), I looked up from my typewriter to see a very tall young man standing at the entrance. I still have a memory of that first sighting of the man I was to marry. We began to go out together on dates some time after Harold started working as a civil engineer for the Board of Water Supply. Harold found when he returned from his Mainland trip that he no longer had a job with the Board of Water Supply. He was able to find a job as civil engineer with Standard Dredging Company.

Harold and I continued to see each other, and finally, on February 26, 1938, we decided to get married. At that time of my life I was not happy about the idea of marriage because I could see that it was not working between my father and mother. Although they never discussed divorce I knew that my father had only one love in his life. She was his cousin Frances, and had refused to marry him because of that close blood tie. I was named for *her*, and that may have been one of the reasons that I never felt a particularly loving relationship with my mother. She probably resented being the second choice, and for me to have her rival's name was perhaps embittering. There was never any open difficulty between her and my father, but I knew love did not reside there.

Anyway, I agreed to marry Harold, and we simply walked out of my home and called a couple of friends as witnesses and went to the home of a minister, who married us. I informed my parents about it after the fact, and they allowed us to take up residence in the little beach house my family owned at Lanikai.

Thinking back, it all seems so cold and matter-of-fact, yet our marriage has so far lasted some sixty years. That's a lot longer than a lot of weddings that start out with white satin gowns and veils and all the "hoop-la" of a traditional wedding.

It was hard on my parents, though. Father told me that when mother learned the news, she cried because she felt so excluded. If I ever meet her in the hereafter, I hope she'll forgive me my lack of understanding.

After we were married we began to put up a little shack on ʻAiea Heights. Harold had previously bought, for a thousand dollars, a one-acre lot on ʻAiea Heights which had a pile of used lumber lying on it. The land sloped in the direction of and had a superb view of Pearl Harbor and the Waiʻanae Range. This superb view of Pearl Harbor was how I came to be probably one of the few remaining witnesses of the whole attack on Pearl Harbor.

Harold found an old Japanese carpenter (who was a drunk), and the two of them managed to put together a little shack with a tin roof which had one big room with a *puneʻe* (movable couch) in it, plus a bathroom and a kitchen. The lot was a "flag lot" reached by quite a long driveway, and there was no electricity available. So we had quite a few cold showers, helped out by a bucket of water heated on our Coleman stove.

Eventually, when we saved enough to afford it, we arranged to have several poles installed down our driveway and we finally had electricity. You cannot imagine the sense of luxury it gave us to be able to turn on a switch and have lights and a hot shower.

At about this time my parents, now that I was married, decided to try living on the Mainland because my mother, after a lifetime of living near mango trees, developed a severe allergy to them. They invited us to move into the family home at Punchbowl so that I would be closer to a hospital, since I was pregnant with my first baby. So we accepted their invitation and moved there. While my parents were on the Mainland, we invited Harold's mother to come to be with us for a while since there was now room for her to visit, which she did. Our son Douglas was born on November 29, 1939, at Kapiʻolani Hospital.

Marie and I suffered the mother-in-law syndrome, unfortunately all too common, which was much aggravated by the fact that she was affronted that we had just gone off and gotten married without due notice to all and sundry. After all, no one could have been good enough to marry her one and only son. It seemed to her that there must have been some ulterior reason for the way we got married.

Also, she was very critical of my family home in which I had grown up. This was a sprawling house which had grown in every direction over the years and did not have a single window you could close! My father had made canvas roll-down curtains which were lowered in Kona storms to protect our large veranda on which we practically lived, and the back of the house was a large screened sleeping porch, also protected by roll-down curtains. What more did anyone need in Hawai`i's benevolent climate?

She was upset by the casual way the house was built. I was particularly fond of the long, wide veranda from which one looked out through a huge, blooming plumeria tree over the city, but the joys of open-air life in Hawai`i escaped her, although actually she and her husband and Harold had lived in Hawai`i enough to know better.

The final blow was when she said to me: "After all, Harold's father is a Virginia gentleman." (Unstated, but implied, Who are *you*?) Rather than point out to her that my father was a master mariner and a ship's captain, whereas her father had been a blacksmith, I descended into a great silence, called *nuha* in Hawaiian, and never broke it until she departed, after the birth of Douglas.

Harold supported me in my feelings, fortunately, or the marriage could have ended right there.

PEARL HARBOR

During the years before the attack on Pearl Harbor, Harold transferred to the Hawaiian Dredging Company and continued to work as a civil engineer for them. There were rumors of war, and there was a great deal of work going on at Pearl Harbor and dredging was part of this. The Hawaiian Dredging Company was part of a consortium of engineering firms employed in improvements at Pearl Harbor.

Harold was at West Loch in Pearl Harbor on the Sunday morning when the Japanese attacked on December 7, 1941. The pressure of work was such that he had felt it necessary to go to West Loch although it was supposedly a day of rest. So he witnessed the attack from a different perspective than I did.

It was about eight o'clock in the morning, and I was at home on 'Aiea Heights, preparing some breakfast for our baby son Douglas, when I heard explosions. When I went to see what was happening it was instantly apparent that Pearl Harbor was being attacked, as from our house we had a perfect view over Ford Island and Battleship Row. Smoke rose up from various parts of Pearl Harbor and Hickam Field and I could see small planes flying low. My first thought was that our house might be attacked and I feared that my baby would be harmed, so I bundled him up in a warm blanket and carried him down the hill and placed him in a large wooden packing crate which happened to be there.

I then went up to the lawn by the house in order to be able to see better. and what I saw filled me with such helpless rage that if I'd had a gun I could have killed. My memories are growing rather indistinct, but I remember seeing the planes making runs to drop their bombs, and already one battleship had turned over at its moorings. Then suddenly the Arizona, which was the one nearest me, erupted in a huge tower of flames.

The scenes of that sunny Sunday morning will remain with me forever. It was devastating to see the destruction and the inability of the Navy to defend itself. Everyone was caught absolutely unprepared.

While I was standing there I was joined by my neighbor. We witnessed a plane flying towards us and we could see the rising sun emblem on its fuselage and the head of the pilot. He swung around at a very low elevation right overhead and started back towards Pearl Harbor, and we heard the sound of his machine gun. I later learned that a bullet had gone through the roof of the house of our neighbors on the downhill side.

Another recollection is of the hospital ship "Mercy," which was anchored off Pearl City Peninsula. It was painted white and had a large red cross on it, which I believe was an international symbol for a hospital ship. I heard machine gun fire and saw a Japanese plane streaking down in flames, firing at the hospital ship. It was hit by bullets from the ship and went down just astern of the "Mercy." I remember screeching with rage at the sight of that plane trying to stretch its fall to crash on the hospital ship.

Not long after this, Frank and Dottie Nott came up the hill from `Aiea Village, to see what all the noise was about. When Dottie surveyed the smoking, blazing catastrophe she turned to me and said, "Well, that's the end of my block-printing business." (She had a home business where she made block prints on fabrics for mu`umu`us and aloha shirts.) I remember being too stunned to reply.

We went into the house and turned on the radio, and to this day have never heard any one else say that they heard the following, but the Notts and I most certainly did. I do not remember what station the radio was tuned to, but there was a man's voice broadcasting "news" that Japanese boats were landing on the Wai`anae coast, and that Japanese planes were approaching from the Diamond Head side. Then the main power switch in Honolulu was cut off by the electric company and we did not hear anything else. This broadcast was obviously meant to frighten the population and although I wrote the Navy about it I never received any response.

When I had time to think about my husband, I remembered that the dredging company's office was at Hospital Point, and felt sure I would never see him again. It was many long hours before he was able to come home. Actually, he had been over in West Loch and had witnessed the attack from there–and was safe because the main thrust was at Battleship Row.

When electric power was finally restored and we were able to hear the radio again the next day, I listened to President Roosevelt's broadcast about the attack and was furious at his belittling of the damage done to Pearl Harbor when the evidence was before my eyes. Of course, I realized it was done in order not to give information to the enemy, but if the nation could have seen what we saw, mobilization might have been even faster.

One other impression remains forever in my mind, and that is the sound of shrapnel whizzing very close overhead. When Hal finally got home, that first day, he and I dug a shallow trench under our house as a refuge (my own private foxhole). He then went back down to Pearl Harbor to do what had to be done, leaving me with the baby and the goat. (More on the goat soon.) The sequence of events is vague now in my mind, but early the next morning some planes arrived from the Mainland and were mistaken for enemy. My somewhat faulty memory is that a warning siren woke me up and I took refuge with baby Douglas in the shallow trench under the house. While I was crouching there, shrapnel began screaming over my head and I instinctively threw myself over my baby's body to protect him. A couple of houses farther up the slope from our place received hits of shrapnel. Fortunately, no one was injured or killed.

The aftermath, with the military in charge, martial law, and blackouts of our houses, while lights were visible in Pearl Harbor (because of the work going on there), and rationing of gasoline and food, was all endurable, but it was a great change from our former carefree way of life.

Because we were in an isolated area and were not able to have milk delivered, we had decided to buy a goat. I had never in my life touched a goat, much less milked one, but we found a nice white nanny, a Saanen, with horns, who was pregnant. A short time after we brought her home she delivered two adorable little white kids. My father built me a little wooden stand with a feed tray and the nanny and I worked out an agreement whereby I would put some barley in the feed tray and she would hop up on the stand and kindly allow me to have some of her milk. I was pretty clumsy at first but we worked out an amicable agreement, and I got a quart and a half of wonderful milk every day, which nourished our son Douglas. My friend, the bacteriologist at the Board of Water Supply, tested the milk and pronounced it superb and safe. Nanny was very responsive to a pleasant conversational tone, and showed her resentment of any rough words by tossing her horns.

Nanny lived in a pen at the bottom of our acre lot and I would have to go down and fetch her up for milking. It was often muddy and I certainly never wore my Sunday best to go and get her. In those days I had hip-length hair, and this morning it was hanging loose. Just as I arrived at the house in my ragged old dress, leading Nanny, a jeep came down our driveway. There were two, pink-cheeked lieutenants in the jeep, their complexions revealing that they had just gotten off a plane. They stopped when they saw me. One of the lieutenants said audibly to the other, "Do you think she speaks English?"

As it turned out, they were seeking locations for machine gun emplacements, and because of the grand view from our lot they had come down our driveway.

Here I should fill in some more information about my husband's life as a civil engineer.

Harold was sent to Midway Island during the war, again for dredging work, but had to be sent back to Hawai`i for recuperation from an operation for appendicitis which had to be done on Midway. Fortunately, there happened to be a physician from the Mayo Clinic on Midway.

During the years he worked for Hawaiian Dredging Company, Harold was sent out on various jobs to Japan and Guam and also traveled to the Mainland on several occasions for the Dredging Company.

LIFE TOGETHER as PARENTS

All parents think their babies are beautiful, but perfect strangers used to stop me on the street to exclaim over Douglas. He was eleven pounds at birth and perhaps because of his weight was slow to begin walking. He finally did at about ten months. He was a smiling baby, with a lot of taffy-colored curls. There was a difficult time in the beginning when adjustments to his diet were being made because I seemed unable to produce enough milk to keep him happy.

He grew up a quiet child, probably rather intimidated by his dominating parents, and did not do well at school, although later in life he began to become a reader and in that way to improve his mind. In the hope that a good school would improve his grades we sent him to the Hawai`i Episcopal Academy in Waimea on the Island of Hawai`i for the last years of high school, where the Headmaster finally told us, "Douglas is a wonderful, sweet boy, a beautiful personality, but he is not college material." He suggested testing him for aptitude, which we had done in Honolulu and discovered that he tested very high in mechanical aptitude.

It is too bad that this testing was not done much earlier–it would have saved all that struggle between a father whose expectations were unrealistic and a son who could only be what his genes made him. He had magnificent physical coordination. I remember one time on the beach at Lanikai when Douglas was a teenager. I was struggling to master a casting rod and becoming very frustrated, when Douglas quietly took the rod and made a perfect cast out to sea on the first try.

His mechanical aptitude got him a job at the airport doing aircraft maintenance on small planes and he was able to take flying lessons. His instructor told me that he was a "natural." He was a good driver too, from a start in the pineapple fields of Kaua`i where I taught him. The only thing I forgot was to show him how to park a car and when we went to get his license at the police station in Līhu`e he flubbed it, so dear old Capt. Waialeale took him out, showed him how and gave him his license.

He married a lovely girl named Diane Moore and they had three daughters. Their three daughters all live on the island of Hawai`i: Cheryl, who married Dwayne Kuilipule; Lisa Leinaala [of "Letter to Lisa"], who married Tyson Jardine; and Kristin Mahealani who at this writing is unmarried and crazy about horses (like me). Lisa and her sisters will have to fill in their side of the genealogy when the time comes.

As a shocking aside, on December 2, 1981, Douglas was killed in a one-car accident on the infamous Saddle Road, which runs up across the plateau between Mauna Kea and Mauna Loa. They were headed up to play in the snow on Mauna Kea. No one will ever know what caused the accident. The car was filled with family, including Stephanie and her boyfriend Tom, who was also killed.

It was one of those turns in our lives that will always be remembered with pain and sorrow. We were able to arrange for Douglas' ashes to be buried at the foot of his Great-grandmother Sarah's grave at Homelani Cemetery in Hilo.

Our daughter Stephanie is a "baby-boomer." I was seized, along with so many others, with the impulse that fueled that boom–the trauma of the attack on Pearl Harbor and the entry into World War II–and an unreasoning human reaction to reassure ourselves that in the midst of death, life would go on. And I wanted a daughter and got one.

She was born in a blackout with her father and mother giggling and lost in the blackout in the hospital car park. I really thought she might arrive before we found the entrance. The hospital was the little one that served `Aiea Plantation and was very homey and friendly.

Stephanie was eleven and a quarter pounds at birth, topping Douglas' eleven pounds. I have chaotic memories of struggling on the delivery table and having to have my arms tied down and cursing the nurses, as a result of the use of the truth serum, which was supposed to suppress pain. Harold was a witness to all this and, as a result, he later decided to have a vasectomy.

Our new baby bore a very strong resemblance to her Polish grandmother and had the palest blond hair, which darkened as she grew older. She was a sprite as a child, with an elfin sense of humor, and was a joy to have around.

She and Douglas grew up at the home we bought in Nu`uanu Valley on Park Street. There are many happy memories of that place, and the two German shepherd dogs we had. I still remember with a smile the day that the children announced that they wanted to dig a swimming pool. We said, "Okay, you can dig one over there," in a patch of dirt where we had not yet landscaped. So they dug for a little while, and uncovered the pancake bank where Heidi, the senior dog, had stashed all the pancakes we had given her. She would come to the door and ceremoniously receive the pancake in her mouth and go away with it, and we thought she had eaten them all–but no, she stashed them in her pancake bank. I believe the swimming pool got about two feet deep before the children gave up the project.

After my marriage and the birth of Douglas and Stephanie, I stayed at home and raised them until they were of an age to become self-sufficient. I tried going back to work at the Board of Water Supply, but gave it up finally because I was getting so wound up in getting two pre-school children dressed, fed, and on the way to Central Union Pre-School from our house in `Aiea Heights that by the time I arrived at work at eight o'clock, it would take me all morning to calm down. Children that age have no conception of time and of course they couldn't understand all the rush. I realized that I was taking out my frustration on them and that it was not good for us, so I regretfully left the work I had enjoyed. I have only sympathy for working mothers who feel they must leave their children for other people to care for.

As the children grew older we began to make an annual trip to the island of Hawai`i. At first we had the privilege of staying at the Hawaiian Dredging Company's vacation house for a couple of weeks at a time, once a year. Originally this was a house within the National Park boundaries. The place was looked after by a wonderful Japanese couple–the wife was the cook-housekeeper, and the husband was the gardener-maintenance man.

Later, the Park decreed that there would be no more private ownership within the Park boundaries, so the Dredging Company bought another house down near "29 miles" on the Hāmākua Coast, where we stayed a few times. Eventually we purchased land at Onomea, the bottom half of a small *ahupua`a* named Pu`umoi, in the Hilo District. It was a natural paradise, bounded on each side by a stream with a seventy-foot high waterfall, the ocean on one side, and the old round-the-island road on the inland side.

Every year while the children were coming into their teens we spent the Christmas holidays over there, camping out in a bunkhouse which we built, with outside cooking and a *hale li'ili'i* (outhouse) with a superb view of Mauna Kea. I remember that we used to be plagued with bees, which during our year-long absence, liked to make their home under the seat of our outdoor toilet. Once when we tried to smoke them out they got annoyed and swarmed all around us. In those days I still had hip-length hair and it was hanging loose, and some bees got trapped in my hair, causing me some desperate moments.

On Sunday mornings we used to tramp into the old Hilo Drug Store for a fancier breakfast than we could prepare at Pu'umoi. We bathed in the streams, and had what I remember as wonderful times there. In later years I often wondered whether the children felt cheated of all the Christmas celebration we missed out on by going camping.

While on Hawai'i we would make excursions to various places on the island. I well remember the time we went up to Mauna Kea. The whole expedition was quite impromptu. We had a jeep which we had shipped over from O'ahu, and we drove up the Saddle Road, turning off at the road which went up quite steeply in places to what was called Hale Pōhaku at 10,000 feet elevation, where there were a couple of stone houses with bunks and very primitive facilities for hikers. Nowadays, of course, there are a number of observatories on top of Mauna Kea because the atmosphere is so clear for viewing.

We had our beloved Heidi, an exceptional dog, along with us and she probably saved Hal and Douglas from hypothermia. It was late morning when we desultorily started up the trail to the summit. Stephanie and I got to about 12,000 feet, at Keanakāko'i, "the cave of the adzes," and suffered such blinding headaches from the elevation that we went no farther.

The mountain was clear of clouds and we had a wonderful, sweeping view of the island. Being above the tree-line, the whole area was bare and desolate except for what appeared to be floating milkweed seeds. We saw no birds. Hal and Douglas persevered and got up to the summit, to the edge of Lake Wai`au. They both had headaches, especially Douglas, but it didn't keep them from going all the way up. The afternoon was getting on and Stephanie and I decided to begin our descent, reaching Hale Pōhaku at 10,000 feet just before sunset. I began to be quite worried as the sun went down and darkness descended. We waited and waited at the beginning of the trail, and finally, in complete darkness, the weary hikers appeared. If Heidi had not been with them to guide them in the darkness, they could have been lost in that mountain cold all night long, without proper warm clothing.

The poor dog was exhausted, with all her exploratory running back and forth, and we picked her up and slung her onto one of the bunks, where she heaved a great sigh and went to sleep. She had worn her paws raw on the rough cinders. The next day she slept all the way home in the jeep with her paws stretched out and her head in my lap. She stepped very gingerly until her paws healed.

The other thing I remember about that Mauna Kea experience was the static electricity which caused my hip-length hair to stand straight out when I attempted to brush it.

Another time we made the descent down Hilina Pali, in Ka`u and camped overnight at a fascinating spot called Halape. This was a little shelter built on a *pāhoehoe* flow, with a delightful, tiny lagoon sheltered from the open sea by a couple of large *pāhoehoe* bubbles. This spot sank into the sea one night in 1975 during a severe earthquake, carrying with it an encampment of Boy Scouts, some of whom drowned. Ka`u has a history of such events.[1] This little spot was a paradise for centipedes–never had I seen so many, and in fact, Douglas was stung by one of them.

The climb back up from Halape was exhausting and I, the great hiker, member of the adventurous Piko Club,[2] was vertically challenged, and just before the top of the trail had to lie down and rest awhile, while my preteens were able to continue up with no problems.

Many years and many travels later, after we returned from East Pakistan the first time, we went back for a visit to Pu`umoi, but Harold's work never seemed to fit in with vacations. Eventually we sold the property to a Hilo doctor who pestered us to sell and kept meeting the absurdly high prices we mentioned casually until we finally sold it to him.

HORSES! MY EARLY LOVE, and an OLD FRIENDSHIP RENEWED

In the early fifties, with Stephanie and Douglas well established in school and Hal in a secure job with Hawaiian Dredging Company, I reentered the world of horses, an early love of mine which had been interrupted by marriage and the war years. A childhood friend, Sheila Dowsett von Geldern, had been given a horse by her cousin, Richard Smart, of the Parker Ranch, and she invited me to ride it. That led to an acquaintance with a real character–Dr. Clarence Fronk who, somewhere near the age of seventy, set himself to purchasing halter-broken thoroughbreds from Parker Ranch and training them for polo. At that time there still existed in Waikīkī, in the back of Kap`iolani Park, a stable which had been there from very early times, perhaps even dating back to the time of the Hawaiian Monarchy. During that period a racecourse had existed at the park and polo was played there regularly.

Riding and caring for Dr. Fronk's untrained horses garnered me my share of falls, but I loved it so much that I took the opportunity to purchase a beautiful thoroughbred mare named Poha. She was a bay and had the most refined conformation and I fell for her looks and disposition, which was quirky–but never did I share a dull moment with this fine mare.

I formed a friendship with Patsy Metcalf, who also kept a horse at the stables, and when the opportunity came for her to buy a very handsome thoroughbred from Jack Burton, a very congenial Army colonel who had been transferred away from Hawai`i, Patsy said she wanted to buy the horse but couldn't afford him. So I offered to go "halfies" with her, and we bought the horse she named Manfredo after an Italian count she had met on one of her travels. Of course no one failed to ask me which end I owned. About Jack Burton, one of my fond memories of him was when he was talking to his little six-year-old son and cautioning him, "Now be careful–one end bites, the other end kicks."

I did not ride Manfredo very often because I did not care for his personality. He was a descendant of Man o' War, a notoriously irascible horse, so I left him to Patsy.

Patsy and I rode together a great deal and were very comfortable with each other. But things changed–the stable closed down after many historic years, and we dispersed with our horses to other stables and pastures. Our lives changed, too, since in a later chapter I'll describe how I went abroad with Hal. Our time spent in East Pakistan intervened, and Patsy and I lost touch with each other.

Jumping ahead in time, in December of 1997, more than thirty years later, when we were living on Kaua`i and contemplating selling our house and moving to a senior complex in Lĭhu`e, I picked a realtor out of the phone book and invited her to come and look at our house with a view to putting it on the market. She was a bright, attractive young woman, and in the way that people born in Hawai`i recognize each other, I knew she was a "local."

We discussed the sale and she offered to write me a letter describing her thoughts and suggestions for the sale, saying it was such a beautiful place. I replied, "I am fortunate to have lived in beautiful places almost my whole life–for instance, I grew up in Lanikai." She looked curiously at me and said, "My family lived in Lanikai a long time ago."

I asked her their name, and when she said Metcalf, I practically shouted: "Then you have got to be Patsy Metcalf's granddaughter."

She called Patsy–whom she calls "Peach"–that very night and left a voice-mail message about our meeting.

It happened that Patsy was coming over to spend Christmas with them, and her granddaughter promised to bring "Peach" to see me. So on Christmas Eve, she and her mother Hattie (who also had moved to Kaua`i unbeknownst to me) brought Patsy for a happy visit. What a nice Christmas present.

MY *KUMU*, MARY KAWENA PUKUI

During the 1950s I was invited to become the social secretary (unpaid, of course) of the membership at the Honolulu Academy of Arts. I accepted, and for a couple of years did volunteer work at the Academy, which I had always loved from my early school days because of the beautiful things to be seen there.

I very much enjoyed an association with Caroline Peterson, who was the very talented volunteer who created the magnificent arrangements which set off the Academy's rooms to perfection. Recently a fine little book with exquisite photographs has been published which describes her work during those years. However, the social committee work palled after a while because when I would invite the ladies who were members of the committee to come and help do something or other for the Academy, they would all show up in their very best clothing, not dressed for, say, lei-making, or moving an exhibit, or something which might get them mussed up.

So for no reason at all (or one of those mysterious coincidences), after I resigned from the Academy of Arts position, I went and volunteered my services as a typist to dear Mary Kawena Pukui, of whom I have fond and respectful memories.

Mary Kawena Pukui was the Hawaiian Scholar at the Bernice Pauahi Bishop Museum at that time. When I offered my services she told me that she would like to have my help, since, she said, "I am a pencil-pusher, not a typist."

I went faithfully to her little office at the Museum, and in typing her translations became entranced with the language. I remember as a child being in the homes of Hawaiian people where there were *kahili* (feather emblems of rank), calabashes, *kapa (tapa)* bark cloth and spears. Nothing like that was found in our home. However, I do have a legacy which I cherish, and that is the bit of my genes which led me to study the Hawaiian language. My studies took a winding course. Seemingly I was meant to learn the language because one step always led to another.

Never let it be said in my presence that Hawaiian is the language of ignorant savages. It has shades of subtleties and meaning, and is

41

an old language which some dedicated people are trying to bring up to date. They have created a whole new lexicon which I am barely familiar with but which is being taught to students. But Kawena Pukui's meticulously written dictionary, which she created with Samuel Elbert, has been an aid to the restoration of the language. My hope is that the new speakers will not lose the humor and the poetic quality of the language. There are so many wonderful metaphors that might be lost if not appreciated by the present-day speakers.

Certainly, my knowledge acquired while typing translations in the Bishop Museum office was my constant aid when I worked at the Hawai`i State Archives as the Hawaiian translator from 1973 to 1976. I kept track of unusual or archaic words or terms, as I worked. I remember being very impressed with the fact that in the entire enormous Native Register of claims made by Hawaiians in the Hawaiian language, which I translated, I came across one little word used in Hilo for a taro patch, which was not used anywhere else in that entire enormous record, and when I looked in the dictionary, there it was!

If not for Mary Kawena Pukui, and a very few others, where would the Hawaiian language be today? That "pencil-pusher" made her mark in the world as a Hawaiian scholar, as her published works show. She was belatedly honored as one of Hawai`i's Treasures.

Perhaps this is the place to say that I was born only fourteen years after the Republic of Hawai`i, formerly the Hawaiian Kingdom, became a Territory of the United States in 1900. People of Hawaiian blood were told that they were now Americans, and that they should speak English, rather than Hawaiian. My mother told me once that she was punished at school for speaking just one Hawaiian word. Others of my mother's generation have told me the same thing.

This may be why my mother never told me anything about my Hawaiian ancestors and I only found out my grandmother's story when I was middle-aged and had gone to do volunteer typing for Kawena Pukui. As I mentioned, I don't know what made me go and offer my services to her, but I do know, in looking back, that our association changed my life because I became fascinated with the Hawaiian language and began to study it on my own. Especially because, as I mentioned earlier, in those days Hawaiian was considered a dead language and very few classes were available where the language could be studied.

I had help along the way, but I started by beginning to acquire a vocabulary which I did by lugging Mrs. Pukui's Hawaiian language dictionary with me wherever I went, even on trips. When I saw a Hawaiian word which intrigued me, I would look it up and so enlarge my vocabulary. I learned enough that I (among others, of course) was able to assist in editing the 1964 edition of the Pukui/Elbert Hawaiian-English Dictionary.

It was Kawena Pukui, whom I consider my Kumu, who told me that my ancestors came from Kaua`i and gave me the name of dear old Helena Kapaka, now long dead, who could give me the genealogical information I wanted.

I also did volunteer work in the Recording Room at the Bishop Museum with Ellie Williamson. She was in charge of all the recordings made of ethnocultural materials, plus all the interviews conducted by Kawena Pukui with informants, on all the islands.

Once I had the good fortune to accompany Kawena and Ellie on a trip to gather information on Moloka`i. When I learned that a trip to Moloka`i was planned, I offered our shack at Honouli Wai as a place to stay. Our place is right on a small, white sand beach, and looks across the channel, only about eleven miles wide, to Maui.

Kawena had interviews with many people scheduled, and she also recorded interviews with people at Honouli Wai. I will always remember the beautiful metaphor used by old Uncle Morris Dudoit, a member of the Dudoit family of Moloka`i. The conversation was all in Hawaiian and I was not yet well enough acquainted with the language to follow it all, but I did hear and understand when he told Kawena, in reference to his age: *"Hele ka la i ka pō, ahiahi no'u,"* which means: The day goes on into night–for me it is evening.

Another happening which fascinates me to this day was a conversation between myself and Peter Black, our next door neighbor of our Honouli Wai property on Moloka`i. Peter lived with Sara Nao`o, who was much older than he was, in her little house right at the point. Peter was the most famous fisherman on Moloka`i, and in fact people were superstitious about him, saying that he had a shark *'aumakua* who protected him in the ocean. The ocean was his supermarket–anything he wanted, he would simply go and get.

One day Kawena decided we should stay home so she could catch up on her notes, so we were all sitting out on the lawn when Peter came over. He was one person whom Ellie was never able to record, since every time he saw her hand reaching out to the Swiss Nagra tape recorder, he would shut his mouth and not say a single word.

I said jokingly to him, "Hey, Peter, how come you're not out fishing on a beautiful day like this?" He replied, "I'm not going in the water today–the *au* (current) is all wrong. Pele is angry." He spoke of the volcano goddess in the most matter-of-fact way. For him, she existed.[1]

And within less than twenty-four hours, in the middle of that night, since we had no telephone in the house, a policeman came and knocked on our door to warn us that there was, indeed, a tsunami alert[2] in effect.

Thinking about Moloka'i reminds me that this island was called *Moloka'i pule 'o'o,* which translates as "Moloka'i of the prayer come to fruition." It was reputed to have most powerful *kahuna* (priest) adepts who could accomplish marvels. The most famous *kahuna* was named Lanikaula, and there are spooky stories told about the celebrated *kukui,* or candlenut tree grove, where he is said to be buried.

I had an experience which made me a believer. It began with my finding an ancient artifact in the sea at Honouli Malo'o Bay. On an evening during a neap tide, Harold and I were prowling the beach looking for artifacts which sometimes washed down the stream onto the beach. The sun was very low on the horizon and I looked up from my search to see what appeared to be a large eye staring at me from out on the water. I immediately waded out to see what it could be, and found it was a large rock with a hole pierced through it, and I recognized it for what it was–an ancient stone canoe anchor.

We were thrilled with our find and filled with the spirit of acquisition, so between the two of us, using a strong piece of pipe inserted through the hole in the rock, we wrestled it into our car and took it to our house at Honouli Wai. Since the original inhabitants were long gone from that area, we felt easy in our minds about taking it. After all, it had shown itself to me. (I can see archaeologists–or pragmatists–shaking their heads over this.)

A very short time after this, I had spotted a stone shrine on the ridge on the Eastern side of Honouli Malo`o Bay. So we took a couple of friends up to see it, and after they and my husband departed down the hill I lingered on, meditating on its use. There were *kī (tī)* plants growing quite near, and I picked a fresh green leaf, laid it respectfully on the stone wall and departed.

Late that night I was awakened by the sound of footsteps made by a large, heavy man going all around our small house. I wondered why Hal was wandering about, but when I reached over I found he was slumbering peacefully at my side. Then I realized that it was impossible to hear such footsteps because the floor was vinyl tile laid on concrete and was very quiet to walk on. So I knew immediately that I was being checked out by a Hawaiian spirit. And the beautiful thing about it was that I felt absolutely no fear. The footsteps had stopped and no harm was meant me, and I knew this.

Our neighbor, Sara Nao`o, Peter Black's wife, whom I remember with much aloha, told me about the time the tidal wave of 1946 washed her house away. She said, "I ran up the hill before the wave got me, and when I looked back, *Auwe!* the wave was taking my house and my *poi* barrel away."

I never went to her house that she did not say to me: "Go eat," an invitation to me to take food in the good old Hawaiian way. She also told me what to do if I ever met a member of the *huaka`i pō*, the night marchers. She said that first I would hear drums and chanting, and when I heard that, I should lie down and cover myself with *mimi* (urine). Next I would hear a voice saying, *"Alia!"* (Stop!) I would be inspected, and the procession would move on.

A friend of ours who had leased some land and built a small vacation house in Hālawa Valley had a strange experience. He and his wife were *haole*, but very much in tune with life in Hawai`i. He was a very pragmatic man who was the president of a dredging firm in Detroit. He told me this story and asked my opinion of it. Late one night he heard frantic knocking on his door. When he went to the window to see who was there he saw a terrified young man beating on his door. The young man begged to be let in because he said "they" were after him. My friend asked, "Who?" The young man replied, "Big men, with feathers and weapons." He was alone and had been camping near the beach at Hālawa Bay.

My friend refused to admit him. After all, his house stood in a very isolated place with no neighbors at all on that far side of Hālawa Stream. He told the young man that he had a rifle right by the door and that he never admitted strangers, but he gave the young man permission to get in his car and sleep there until daylight, which the young man did.

The next morning, which happened to be a Sunday, he gave the young man a lift part way back to Kaunakakai and advised him to report his experience to the police. He described this experience to a very experienced Hawaiian scholar named Zelie Sherwood. Zelie told him that the timing was right for such a thing to happen since it was *Pō Kāne*, the night of the god Kāne, which is the dark of the moon. In ancient Hawaiian belief, this is also the time of the *huaka'i pō*.

RIDING a NEW PATH

When Kawena Pukui retired from the Bishop Museum in the early 1960s after about twenty-five years, a fortuitous opening occurred at the Science Center's Planetarium there, so instead of leaving the Bishop, I was able to get the job of Administrative Assistant to the Astronomer. That was the beginning of a happy friendship with George and Marie Bunton. George was at that time the Astronomer and Manager of the Bishop Museum Planetarium. I told George I should pay him for the privilege of having such a prestigious title (for a mere typist-receptionist). My work consisted of typing letters or other material that George might need, plus admitting people to the regularly scheduled planetarium shows. My office was in the basement of the Planetarium, and I had the duty of taking phone calls as well. Many of them were about astronomical events. Later on during one of the Museum's more poverty-stricken times, I was put on half-time and Marie shared the job with me (with no charge to the Museum). It was a happy, seamless arrangement and we took over from each other with never a problem.

Since my duties for the Planetarium were very light, George allowed me to do translating work on material furnished by the Anthropology Department. I did quite a good deal of work on the historical account of Kamehameha I, written about 1905 by Poepoe.

I also was asked by Marion Kelly, then Senior Anthropologist Kenneth Emory's assistant, to translate some letters relating to a census taken by the missionaries in 1835. My translations ended up as part of a Bishop Museum Bulletin written by Robert Schmidt, the State statistician, entitled, "The Missionary Census of 1835." This was not the first time my name appeared in connection with a publication, as I received credit for assisting in the preparation of the 1964 English-Hawaiian version of the Pukui-Elbert English-Hawaiian Dictionary.[1]

I had learned the Hawaiian language essentially on my own, although there were lucky breaks and help along the way. For instance, I had the opportunity to take over a job from a Hawaiian friend who was assisting Kulamanu Williams to write a book entitled, *Teach*

Yourself Hawaiian. Kulamanu was a member of a *kama'āina* (long time) missionary family who had no Hawaiian blood, but she was extremely interested in the language. I went to her lovely home at the seashore every week day for almost a year to type for her.

Unfortunately, Kulamanu had very bad eyesight and wore thick glasses which didn't help her very much. She insisted on doing the proofreading of the final copy; the result was that some typographical errors crept in which, of course, I did not see. She went ahead and had the book printed at her own expense and, when she discovered the errors, she had the entire issue destroyed.

And that was the end of a year in which I learned enough so that Dr. Sam Elbert allowed me to audit his advanced class in Hawaiian literature at the University of Hawai`i. He knew me because of my work on the English-Hawaiian Dictionary and he didn't care that all I had was a high school diploma. At that time there were five of us in his class. Nowadays, hundreds of young people are learning the language. It has been a remarkable comeback of a language that almost died.

`elua / two

TRAVELS with HAL

1950s to 1960s

COMINGS and GOINGS

Somewhere in these years–the late 1950s and early 1960s–Harold and I took a couple of trips. One of them was to Tahiti, which landed us there right at the beginning of the Fête (Bastille Day). Harold was sent there to estimate a dredge fill to make a landing place for airplanes, as Papeete had no airport. It was served by flying boats that landed on the lagoon at Fa`a`a.

The trip there was memorable and I am still convinced that going by flying boat is the only civilized way to fly. We flew from Honolulu by regular airline to Fiji, landing at Nadi, and drove across the island to Suva, where we spent the night. The next morning we embarked on the Tasman Empire Airways Ltd. (TEAL)[1] flying boat, which was very spacious and comfortable. When we took off the cabin sank below the water level and we could see the green water rushing by the windows until finally we broke free and started to climb.

The whole travel experience was so leisurely and enjoyable. People who have flown only coach class can have no idea of the luxury such a flight afforded. The steward plied us with superb New Zealand sherry and comforted us with apples and other good things. We stopped in Western Samoa to refuel and drove in to Apia for a period of rest at Aggie Grey's hotel. In the middle of the night we were collected and driven back out to the place where the plane was moored, and again went rushing through the water, this time in complete darkness except for a couple of blazing buoys made out of kerosene tins.

The next morning, in a spectacular sunrise, we descended to land on the lagoon at Aitutaki in order to refuel again before the last leg of the journey to Tahiti. It was pure poetry.

As a grand and glorious climax to this journey–truly it is better to travel than arrive–the captain of the plane made a huge sweep completely around Moorea before going in to land at Tahiti. The Fête was all we had heard and more, and was done for the people themselves, not for tourists. It was the real thing, and we enjoyed it all.

Later, when the airport was finished, some Honolulu business men organized an all-male holiday flight to Tahiti. It ended up being called the "First Fornication Flight." I remember that one of my polo-playing friends (reputed to be quite a Romeo) was astonished when he learned that Hal had taken me to Tahiti. But Hal said, "You'd never believe I behaved myself if I didn't take you along." Such were the ways of Tahiti.

Another trip we took together was to Japan, where Hal was asked to go on business. We stayed at a very nice, private home on Legation Hill owned by a man named Ed Shay, who had a business called Pacific Architects and Engineers. Ed was married to a lovely half-Japanese, half-Russian woman; they had one young son and a baby. He had a great deal of regard for Harold because once, during the Korean war, when they both found themselves in Korea, on a very cold night, Harold shared the only bed left in the hotel. Ever after, Ed was Harold's good friend.

During our visit, Ed asked Harold to go on an errand to Manila for him. While he was away, I got brave enough to venture out alone in Tokyo, that fascinating city. I always had the address of Shay's home in my pocket and could take a taxi back when I'd had enough exploration time.

We had never been to the Kabuki Theatre, so one day we went and bought tickets for that day's show, which started in the morning. The tickets were rather expensive, but we had heard that the show went on all day and into the night, so we thought we would get our money's worth. The play as it unfolded was beautiful and fascinating, but when what we thought was an intermission finally came, I had begun to feel unwell, so we decided to leave then, especially because we were leaving Japan early the next morning for home.

In the lobby of the theater we ran into Adek, a Jewish professor who came from Acre, now called Akko in modern Israel. He also was a guest of the Shays. He was a most interesting and lively and intelligent man who spoke eleven languages. Thinking that our theatre tickets were still good, we pressed our stubs on him and urged him to use them to see the rest of the show. He accepted them, and we went on home.

We did not see Adek again until he stopped in Honolulu a few days later and phoned us. Stephanie and I took him to lunch, and he told us the end of the story of the Kabuki performance. It seems that when the usher looked at his ticket stubs, he was baffled and confused because there were people seated in what had been our seats. So the usher called the manager, who came and in perfect English asked Adek, "Sir, may I ask where you got these tickets?" This was the moment that Adek gave him a complete explanation in very fluent Hebrew, and the manager threw up his hands and had a chair brought for him so he could see the performance.

CULTURE SHOCK in EAST PAKISTAN

In our situation at home in Hawai'i, a man was put in over Harold whom he detested. He quit the Hawaiian Dredging Company and went into business as a contractor for himself. At about this time the opportunity came to work in East Pakistan, as it was then called. Now it is Bangladesh. Harold had suffered a financial loss on a contract to build the small-boat harbor at Port Allen on Kaua'i. Here was a chance to earn tax-free money and recoup our fortunes, and so he took the job and left for East Pakistan.

By that time our children were old enough to be on their own, so Douglas was established in the trailer which we had in our Nu'uanu garden, where my parents had lived, and I set Stephanie up in our house at Lanikai, with our dear Shepherd dog 'Ele to protect her (I thought). Little did I know what a burden I was placing on poor Stephanie by saddling her with the dog. I was then able to rent our house on Park Street in Nu'uanu Valley.

We thought it was more important to have Stephanie finish her studies at the University of Hawai'i than to come with us to East Pakistan, which was a real hardship post, with no available educational opportunities. In retrospect I know we should have taken her to Pakistan, where she would have gotten a real education. I believe it would have given her a broad perspective on life that she could have obtained in no other way. But who knows– she might have ended up hating us for dragging her out to that place where there was really nothing for a girl her age to do. And also, it was a Muslim country where females were not free to move about. We always wanted to do the right thing, but will never know whether we did.

Having arranged for Stephanie's place to stay, I proceeded to empty the house of fifteen years of accumulation at Park Street in Nu'uanu Valley where we had moved after we sold our acre of land and shack on 'Aiea Heights. I then arranged to rent the main house, while Douglas lived in the trailer in the garden.

I believe that if Americans could have the experience of living in a hardship post such as East Pakistan was and is, they would get their priorities straight.

It was a revelation to me since, except for the trips to Tahiti and Japan, and a 65,000 mile journey across the country by car and trailer with my father in 1936 which included a jaunt from San Francisco down to Mexico City–a real adventure by car at that time–and a trip around the Gaspè Peninsula at the mouth of the St. Lawrence River, I had no real travel experience. (A more complete description of this trip is included in the description my father wrote in his "Journal and Ships' Log" in the "Travels" section.)

It was my good fortune to have grown up in Hawai'i in a multicultural society, so I had felt no doubts at all about my ability to live happily in East Pakistan. I thought I would fit right in to the new life.

But I was wrong because my impressions about life in India were colored by my reading of Kipling's *Jungle Book* and *Kim*. I was unprepared for the grim poverty and the dirt. And worst of all, I was unprepared for life in a Muslim country.

Harold had gone ahead of me by six months. He arranged for a house for us to live in while I prepared to leave Douglas and Stephanie and rent our house. On advice from Harold, I shipped out a large crate of canned foods since he wrote that such things were expensive and hard to come by. In any event, the crate did not arrive for six months after I arrived in Dacca, and by then we had learned to live on the food of the country, and had become addicted to curry.

In order to get to Dacca I had to fly to Calcutta, half-way around the world. We landed at the Dumdum airport at Calcutta in the late afternoon, and the drive in to Calcutta was an eye-opener for me, as the whole way was lined with homeless people preparing to go to sleep in their rags along the route. There were cooking fires with people huddled around them, and hordes of small children. The sight was so depressing that when I arrived at the hotel in Calcutta, I went to my room, wedged a chair against the door and went to bed, foregoing my own dinner.

Next morning it was back to the airport for the short flight to Dacca. It was in the beginning of the monsoon season; the country we flew over was practically all under water from the floods. I could not imagine where we would land in that watery world. There was water everywhere, with just mounds visible here and there, and perhaps a mango tree and a hut on each of them. The railroad lines and main highways were up above the flood on causeways, and temporary houses were on stilts all along the causeways.

I was met at the Dacca airport by Harold and some of the people he worked with, whose names I have now forgotten. I was startled at Harold's appearance–he had lost a great deal of weight; the skin was hanging on his bones, because of almost constant attacks of dysentery. When he was at home under controlled conditions, where the drinking water was sterilized at a rolling boil thirty minutes, and the food was carefully prepared, he would be all right. But whenever he had to go into the field, he would get sick.

In connection with the dysentery, I remember a conversation I had with Quaneta, a very nice young Pakistani woman who lived across the alley from us–more about her later. Quaneta said to me, "I don't understand why all you Americans make such a fuss over boiling the water." I explained to her how vulnerable we were to the microscopic creatures that inhabited the water, soil and air of that country, and I forbore to say to her that, after all, the life expectancy in her country at that time was less than half than that in the U.S.

That first evening in Dacca, Harold took me for a ride in his little "Deux Chevaux" to purchase some bread, so I got a good look at the place where I was destined to live for more than two years. It was very dismaying and strange, distinctly "un-Hawai`i," and when a poor ragged old man came up to my car window and started begging for *baksheesh*, I dissolved into tears and cried off and on for almost two weeks, which was very unlike me. Poor Harold was at his wit's end to comfort me, and as a last resort he began to teach me to play cribbage, which was the beginning of a life-long tournament.

Ever since, playing cribbage together has been an almost daily part of our lives. Which reminds me of something that happened in later years when we were on the island of Hawai`i. We decided to treat ourselves to a couple of nights at the Volcano House. The Volcano House, high in Volcanoes National Park on the island of Hawai`i, was a world-famed establishment. Its host was a Greek named George

Lycurgus. His cribbage games with famous people were written up in the Honolulu newspapers.

We sat in the bar and played cribbage while we had our drinks. "Uncle" George, who had by then died, had been celebrated for his gallantry to the ladies, and I felt especially favored that evening by Uncle George because it was impossible for me to lose. I even knew what cards were going to be turned up. An experience like that (especially if you are Hawaiian), can make a person believe that there are indeed 'aumakua, or guardian spirits watching and guiding you– even during a cribbage game.

Back to Dacca and my culture shock: Finally, one day, a delegation of young American wives of employees of our company came to see me, and offered to teach me to play bridge. I was of the opinion that women who sat on their fannies around a bridge table were a pretty useless bunch, but thank goodness I withheld that opinion and agreed to try to learn, and loved it! I will always be beholden to Darlene and Sarah, two really sweet, heads-up young women. We spent many happy hours at each others' houses and with others in the group of Americans and English in Dacca.

The Pakistani women were all avid mah-jong players, and kept to themselves. I always thought it was too bad we couldn't all somehow get to know each other, but it never happened--the gulf was too great. Except for my friendship with Quaneta.

Of course, I never got to the top in the bridge circle–but I did make a few grand slams with the accompanying thrill. There were a couple of women who were simply awesome in their ability to know where every card was at all times. They had their own little group of experts but they would very kindly consent to make an occasional fourth in our duffer group. I will always remember Mimi Beeson, a young Hong Kong Chinese who belonged to the "good" players. Her husband was a tea planter in the hill country North of Dacca. Whenever we were partners and I got the bid she would say in her very British accent, "Well, 'Frawnces,' I'd better go to the restroom and light a joss stick now."

Our house was set in a short alley occupied by only two houses. Ours was a small two-story house. Our ground floor flat had one bedroom, with quite a large living room and a beautiful terrazzo floor. The upstairs flat was occupied by an American master mechanic employed at the dredge base. His wife was Russian and was quite a character. She used to go out, in the daytime when her husband was at work, in a closed rickshaw with a very suspicious looking fellow. For all I knew they might have been spies. She must have had some reason for sticking around with a man who beat her pretty regularly, as our servants delighted to inform us.

We had a rather unusual mix of servants. Compared with other foreign residents in Dacca, we were very conservative and employed only three men. Other residents employed as many as ten, and if they didn't have enough servants they would borrow from their neighbors whenever they put on a "ten-boy" curry dinner. At one of those parties, when it came time to serve dinner, there would be a file of men waiting to enter the dining room, and they would each be carrying a tray of separate condiments for the curry. Quite a social splash!

There was a convention that in order to avoid strife the servants must all be of the same religion. By contrast, we had a mix of disparate religions: the cook was Buddhist, the bearer was Christian and the gardener, called a *mali*, was Muslim. The *mali* was extremely devout: the first thing we heard in the morning was the prayers recited as he did his first of the five obligatory prayers of the day. The bearer oversaw the household and served meals and prepared drinks from the locked storage *godown,* or shed (to which we kept the key).

The cook also did the marketing because women (both foreign and Pakistani) did not go to the market. The *mali's* job was the care of the garden and keeping the car clean. The cook found a young boy who did the washing and for all we knew, slept with the cook. The first boy whom the cook brought to the house got sick. When we took him to Dr. Bassett, the doctor told us he had almost every kind of known intestinal parasite, and he had to worm him like a puppy.

In spite of the religious differences, the servants shared the servants' quarters quite harmoniously, as far as we knew, although space was limited.

DAILY LIFE in DACCA

I had shipped my English saddle out to Dacca because I had hoped to be able to continue riding, but this was not practicable. For a short time, by arrangement through a friend, I went every morning to a police stable to join their morning exercise circle. The mounted police were important for crowd control and they kept their mounts in good condition, but the walk-trot-canter routine in a rather small circle was boring.

One morning (it was November 22, 1963) while I was riding there, they came to me and told me that they had just received the news of President Kennedy's assassination. I was numb with shock–it seemed to me that the United States had just become as lawless as any other part of the world. This news shook the foundations of my sense of security.

My experiences in Dacca and stories related to me of others' experiences had already shown me how precarious life in that part of the world could be.

When Hal first arrived in Dacca, his boss was a man named Paul Enright, who was not in very good health by the time that I arrived. When he was forced to leave because of his health, he sold us his little English-make car, with the right-hand drive, and I learned to drive it so that I could visit the homes of my friends. The traffic on the road was extremely dangerous because of the mix of people, cars, trucks loaded with bricks, ox-carts, to say nothing of the occasional roaming animal. At least, this being a Muslim country, there were no privileged cows roaming freely as they do in Calcutta, since to Hindus they are sacred.

Gasoline for the car was not easy to get and was of very poor quality, and affected the function of the car. One day I decided to go into the Old Town to a bazaar where I made a few purchases. When I got back to my car it would not start, so I motioned to a couple of men sitting on an ox-cart for help. With that, a swarm of boys descended on us and a mob started to push. Finally the engine started up and they began to clamor for baksheesh and were beginning to climb all over the car. Reaching into my purse, I grabbed all my loose change and flung it out of the window and got out of there while they were scrambling for the money.

I had heard stories of how a bus driver who had run over a child had been torn to pieces by a mob who also demolished the bus.

The only other reason I had for going to the Old Town was that several of us American women had offered to assist Pamela Klausner in her clinic for women, which had been set up by the Society of Friends. This clinic was in a part of Old Town which was appalling to see. People lived on the dirt in shelters thrown together out of matting, flattened kerosene tins, anything they could drag together. Some of the women who came to the clinic were shivering with malaria, and all of them lived in the twilight world of malnutrition.

We were to learn how to make injections (practicing how to insert the needle on an orange!) and assist the Hindu woman doctor (of course, a male doctor was out of the question). She would examine a woman and prescribe something, and if it was an injection, one of us, having learned the "sterile routine," would do it. I was disgusted by the scornful manner of the doctor–she seemed totally lacking in sympathy.

Our efforts to do good ended when a vast riot spread over the entire sub-continent at the episode of the "hair of the Prophet." At a mosque in Kashmir, more than a thousand miles away, a holy relic said to be a hair of the Prophet's beard disappeared. Immediately there was an outcry and Hindus were blamed for the theft. Whole villages were mobbed and the inhabitants murdered. The rivers were full of bodies. Hal, whose work was on the river, can testify to this.

We foreign women were ordered to stay within our compound walls, as it was entirely too dangerous to be out. There was a Hindu potters' village only a mile or so away from our house, and a mob attacked that village one night. We heard the roar of the crowd and the screams and it left me with an extreme dislike ever after of being in the midst of any kind of crowd.

Finally, after things settled down again, we made another visit to the Friends' clinic, and found that in our absence the few Pakistani women volunteers had not gone there either, and everything in the clinic was dirty and the sterile equipment was covered with mildew.

So we gave up our efforts and went back to the bridge table, because the hope had been that our efforts would encourage more Pakistani women to volunteer. But they could apparently not overcome their home-bound culture.

When we first planned to go to East Pakistan we visited a doctor we knew for some shots.

When he heard where we were going he said: "So you're going to East Pakistan? Would you like to see how many diseases are endemic there?" And he showed us a long, long list. So we had our preventive shots and took our malaria pills while we were in the country. We boiled the water at a rolling boil for thirty minutes, refrained from eating anything raw, and managed to survive without getting sick too often, although, as I've mentioned, Hal would get sick every time he went out in the field. He finally had an attack of amoebic dysentery, which had to be cured with arsenic. We used to joke that if ever he died in suspicious circumstances, someone (probably me) would be suspected of having poisoned him.

There was an English doctor who looked after the foreign community, and there was the Holy Family Hospital–a gleaming oasis of cleanliness and hope. The hospital had been built by the Catholic Medical Mission sisters themselves, and they kept it in immaculate order, compared to the dirt and dishevelment of the surrounding country.

There were stories about the other hospital–a place to be avoided at all costs. I remember being told one story about a patient too weak to reach for his food (supplied by his family) and too weak to chase off the crows which hopped in the open window and ate it all.

The Pakistani government had suffered the Catholics to build this hospital in Dacca, and also there was a small Seventh-Day Adventist hospital (which I never visited). But I heard that after the partition between East Pakistan and West Pakistan,[1] the government took over the hospital and expelled the nuns.

The poverty and malnutrition were difficult for the people to endure at any time, but during Ramadan, the important Muslim festival held from September to October, it was even more difficult. The calls to prayer were no longer a musical call by a muezzin from the minaret, but a blaring loudspeaker, and during Ramadan there was additional noise from a siren which would go off early enough in the morning to warn people to get up and prepare their meal before the sun rose to where a white thread could be distinguished from a black one. All during the daylight hours it was forbidden to partake of food or drink, and the rickshaw men, especially, suffered.

I still have a mental picture of a man dazed by malnutrition who was carrying a shoulder yoke with two pails of yogurt. He stepped down off the sidewalk right into an oncoming taxi which caught one end of the shoulder yoke and spun the man around in a spiral of yogurt.

I was in the habit of taking a morning walk with a friend who lived across the Dacca "lake," which was actually a sewage lagoon. One morning as I was returning home, I was appealed to in Bengali by a woman with a baby who was sitting under a tree near our little alley. I thought of going and getting a little *baksheesh* for her, but when I got into the house the servants were all assembled waiting for me. They informed me that the *mali's* wife had been attacked, she and the baby had been beaten, and they had been thrown off the little homestead which the *mali* had earned by his labors in Dacca. This little homestead where the wife lived was down near the port of Chittagong, and she had found her way to Dacca to see her husband. And she was the woman sitting under the tree.

When I heard this I was indignant and said to them: "What in the world are you waiting for, bring her in here!" And with that the *mali* got down on the floor and kissed my feet and wept real tears over them.

His wife was covered with bruises and the baby was an unspeakable sight with great purple bruises all over his body. We took the baby to see Dr. Bassett, and he clucked his tongue but said, as far as he could tell, there were no internal injuries.

I was so upset about this attack on the wife and child that I asked for an interview with our neighbor, who was a Pakistani High Court judge (who, by the way, later became the first President of Bangladesh). His reaction to this sad story was most disappointing. He said to me, "Well, in the first place, we don't know the actual truth of all this. Maybe the place was not actually owned by the *mali*." And he did not think the plight of the woman was at all unusual or that it merited any investigation at all. This was the first of many times that I thanked the Powers that Be that I was born in Hawai`i instead of in a Muslim country, where a woman is as the dirt beneath a man's foot (or as it says in the Koran, "a field to be plowed"), as far as any consideration is given her.

The house across the way was larger than ours, and was occupied by this judge and his family, consisting of his wife and two nieces. They all spoke very good English and were well educated. Quaneta was one of those nieces. Despite our many differences, we formed a friendship, as mentioned before. Her sister, named Saliha, was older and was soon to be married, and I did not have much contact with her.

East Pakistan was Bengali country, different from the inhabitants of West Pakistan. Although there were rabid *mullahs* who inveighed against the freedom granted to women, most of the upper class women did not wear the veil, and those women wore the *shalwar-kameez*, loose pants and a tunic, with a long, draped scarf called a *dupatta*, which could be arranged to hide their features if a strange man came to the house. *Saris* were also worn, of course, on occasion. However, the *burqa*, the enveloping outer garment which hid a woman's face and whole body, was to be seen on the streets here and there.

The customary garb for the men (those who were not westernized) was the *lunghi* wrap and a *kurta*, a long shirt worn hanging out. I would see the men at the edge of the reservoir washing their *lunghis* and draping them over a rock to dry.

The women were confined mostly to their homes, and I was amazed to find that grown women kept collections of dolls very carefully displayed in their living rooms. Women did not go to the markets–that was the job of the cook or the bearer. Also, at social events, the sexes were strictly segregated, and it was a bore to have to attend any function because there was no scintillating conversation. I used to think the women were muzzled because of being kept within their walls. Of course amongst themselves they had plenty to talk about concerning their home lives and family and friends. But for most of them, I might as well have been from another planet and they displayed no curiosity as to where I came from.

With one exception, and that, again, was Quaneta. She worked as a teacher at the English school in Dacca and had an inquiring mind. She had been educated in Calcutta before the Partition[2] in a very good English school. We had a couple of friends in common–they were Bernard and Pam, who ran the Friends' Rescue Service which had been set up in the Old Town in Dacca after the Partition when there was such terrible hardship. Bernard was Swiss and Pam was English, and I was very fond of them and impressed by the ease with which they operated in that strange country.

Bernard and Pam invited Quaneta to accompany them to a meeting of some sort in Hong Kong, and she very much wanted to go, but she came to me in doubt and confided that she was afraid to go because she knew that the Chinese cooked with <u>pork</u> (her emphasis). I became very stiff, and said that I thought it would be a great loss of a valuable experience if her inquiring mind could not figure out a solution to this problem. So she went, and when she returned, she came over and whispered with a smile, "The food was delicious."

The Muslim abhorrence of pork and strict rules excluding anything derived from a pig from their diet and life practices caused a problem at the dredger base at Narayanganj–even by way of reference. A new dredge captain arrived from the USA, and not being adequately indoctrinated in the culture of the country, looked over the dredge he was to work on and said to the crew: "Clean this place up–It is a pigsty." To a man the crew walked off the dredge and reported to Mahmoud, the Director, that the new captain had called them pigs and that they would not work with him. The captain immediately became *"persona non WAPDA"* (Water and Power Development Agency), and had to leave.

Quaneta was also a close friend of Jane–the wife of the young director of the Cholera Lab sponsored by the World Health Organization. Jane had two small children and Quaneta helped Jane to care for them. Jane suddenly developed an aneurysm of the brain and had to be flown on a mercy flight to New York, but she died before arrival. Before she left, she implored Quaneta to look after the children, so she stayed every day at Jane's home and cared for the children.

It was all very traumatic, and Jane's husband, a very intelligent and charming man, did not realize the jeopardy Quaneta was placing herself in until Quaneta's uncle, the judge, called him in for a meeting and said to him, "My niece has been compromised by staying at your house to the extent that she will never be able to find a husband. What do you plan to do about it?"

So a *mullah* was called, and a Muslim marriage ceremony was performed not two months after Jane died.

I wish I could say that they lived happily ever after but I have lost touch with them. They did live together very harmoniously for several years, and Quaneta had a child with him. In fact they visited us when they passed through Hawai`i one time, and Quaneta actually put on a bathing suit and went for a "dip"–couldn't swim, of course, but enjoyed the water enormously. That was quite a leap for a young woman reared in the severe restrictions of the Muslim religion.

Quaneta was quite patriotic, and I often wondered if she had returned to Bangladesh when the partition between West and East Pakistan took place.

The organization Harold was hired to work for was called EP (East Pakistan) WAPDA (Water and Power Development Agency). Since Harold was a dredge expert, he was hired to be the opposite number of a Pakistani engineer named Mahmoud, who managed the dredge fleet in East Pakistan, at a base in Narayanganj, fourteen miles South of Dacca, the capital city of East Pakistan. The dredges were used to keep the navigable waterways open, as the annual floods emanating from the Himalayas often silted up the waterways. After the British Raj departed from India and Pakistan following Independence in 1947, the dredge fleet had deteriorated badly from lack of maintenance, and many of the waterways were no longer navigable.

PAKISTAN DIARY EXCERPTS

November 5, 1963

Day by day the weather is getting cooler, which is very fortunate because I spent the last two days reorganizing and rearranging the kitchen and cleaning and defrosting the refrigerator.

On Monday Munto was late for breakfast, and having been warned this was his last chance, he was fired by Yrs. Truly.

The freezer was completely frosted up and full of unidentifiable packages, so I pitched in and did an honest days work after all this time of taking it easy and being a memsahib. I hope I have solved the problem of why the freezer kept frosting up. Munto was unbelievably careless in not keeping the door closed, with the inevitable result. As an aftermath of my cleanup I discovered one of my good damask napkins had apparently been used as a wiping rag, so it was time he was fired, anyway.

The indent key on the little Olivetti typewriter has jammed; only hope someone in this town can fix it.

On Friday I had lunch at Ruth Downing's, and Pamela Klausner was there. I had arranged to go down to the Friends' Centre with her and Miss Ahmed to see what it was like.

Miss Ahmed is my neighbor, a very bright and friendly young Pakistani woman who teaches at an elementary school in Dhanmandi and who volunteers her time on Friday afternoon to teach an arts and crafts class at the Friends' Centre.

I probably would never have met the people next door if I had not sent a note over addressed to "The Lady of the House," offering her some of our Hawaiian solo papaya seedlings. She speaks little or no English and so sent her niece over to express her thanks and acceptance.

Miss Ahmed is afflicted with a case of what ailed my childhood chum Sheila von G. I believe it is called vitiligo, a lack of pigmentation in areas of her skin including her face. She may never have an arranged marriage which is a great pity because she loves children and enjoys teaching them. She has undergone treatment but it has not seemed to help.

My afternoon at the Centre was interesting. First we went to the new compound which is being built by the municipality and which contains an office, a library, classrooms, and a clinic where 30 mothers at a time can bring their babies. A woman doctor takes care of them, and twice a week a male doctor sees any men who want to come. When we arrived the porch of the kindergarten dispensary building was full of squatting sari-clad mothers and their small children and babies.

The district of Azimpur is very poor (not that the others are not) and when I asked Pamela if that was why they had started the Centre there she said no, that the chairman of this district, or union, just happened to be the only such chairman who displayed an interest in improving the lot of the people. He was a sort of hereditary holder of office, being a landholder in the area whereas the other chairmen were out and out politicians.

From the compound we went to the house where the Klausners live, a biggish 2-storied building set in a large walled compound. The women's sewing shop is there and Pam showed me samples of their handiwork: Embroidered place mats, napkins and bridge cloths and little girls' dresses, all smocked, fagoted, etc. The quality of the work and design was far superior to anything I had yet seen. A Mrs. Khan is the supervisor and she really has good ideas.

The house is set on the edge of a slum; originally the area was dotted with large houses belonging to the landowners, set in immense estates, all of which have now been crammed with bamboo huts thatched with straw, or else tin-roofed. There are huge old trees which take some of the curse off the slumminess, but it is pretty sad-looking.

Pam took me up on the roof so I could see the view and it was an interesting sight from up there, with mosque minarets sticking up through the surrounding trees which at that elevation hide the squalor underneath. Quite near at hand is the huge stone arch of the ruined Mughal fort called Lalbagh, which I hope to get to see.

The everlasting crows, kites and vultures were wheeling overhead and a big black thundercloud kept threatening rain but we had a cup of tea up there on the roof without getting sprinkled on. I should mention here that the same Indian mynahs that one sees in Hawai`i are here very low in the ornithological social scale, so they only utter modest little peeps, not the brassy squawks heard from the mynahs in Hawai`i.

Bernard is starting a carpenter workshop in the garage and plans to take six 12-year old boys who are now working in factories and pay their wages so they can be trained to use tools and maybe learn to design better furniture than the crude articles seen everywhere.

Miss Ahmed told me of a sad experience she had a while back, illustrating an aspect of the government policy. She and ten other young people had made all their arrangements including passports and visas, to take part in the "Experiment in International Living." [I do not remember the source of this "experiment."] They were actually at the airport when they were prevented from leaving by government officials who apparently never had any intention of allowing them to leave.

***

November 7, 1963

I have a new servant who appears to be a pretty fair cook and tomorrow night is going to be my first dinner party. Heaven only knows how it will go. Since Mr. Enright, Hal's boss, lives upstairs, we are trying to work out an arrangement to share his sweeper and all the details have not yet been worked out. I have already been propositioned for an alarm clock and the next thing will probably be a request for new uniforms.

The other day I saw a large advertisement in the newspaper which asked the public to report any cases of corruption to the special officer in charge of anti-corruption. It is the practice here to bribe officials for everything, and the government is allegedly trying to stop this practice. I still wonder if the trouble Darlene Neilsen had in trying to mail two packages at the main post office could have been expedited by a little cumshaw. She sure got the merry old run-around.

On Sunday the Neilsens stopped by and invited us to ride down to Narayanganj as Leroy wanted to buy his month's quota of Scotch at the Narayanganj Club. I had not been to Narayanganj as I had not had the heart to ask Hal to drive me after having to make the daily 28-mile trip. The road is a high causeway with rice paddies stretching away on either side and small villages and finally a glimpse of the Buriganga River with large cargo boats and launches. We passed a match factory and textile mill, and also one area where hundreds of strips of cotton cloth were hung along the roadside, some white and some dyed in violent colors.

We stopped at the Narayanganj club for a beer. The small bar was full of English men and women all having a Sunday morning eye opener. We felt very alien; no one spoke to us.

Afterwards, driving through the narrow old streets I saw several blind men and cripples, and one poor man who had an enormous tumor under one arm from under his shoulder blade around to the front.

In addition to the afflicted humans there was a sad old 3-legged horse, whose near hind leg had recently been cut off just below the hock and he was unconcernedly grazing by the roadside.

We passed the government chicken farm which reminded Leroy of the time he went there to buy some eggs. The man in charge said "Not open for business." So then he went and put a shirt on and opened up a little shack, stuck his head out the wicket, and said "What can I do for you?" It's got to be funny, else it would be infuriating.

We visited an interesting old Mughal fort which was built about 300 years ago to keep the Portuguese pirates from raiding up the river.

***

INDIA (with border countries)

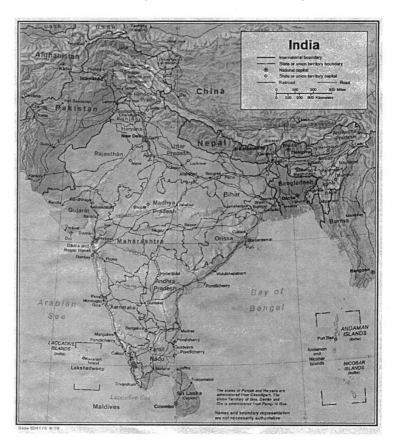

FURTHER TRAVELS

LAHORE

One of the American women I met in Dacca was also a "horse person," and we arranged to fly together to Lahore in West Pakistan to see the annual agricultural show which boasted of its famous white "dancing horses." We flew to Lahore and attended the event, which was a great disappointment, as to the "dancing horses." The horses were indeed white, but their performance was obviously produced by pain, not by the meticulous training of dressage. Their movements were very jerky and ungraceful. We witnessed this at quite a distance as we were seated in a grandstand and the horses appeared on the opposite side of the field, but it was obvious that the horses were not happy performers.

However, the evening military tattoo by torchlight was most impressive, especially the hundreds of bagpipers, all Pakistani, of course, who marched in formation, in Scottish kilts and played the wild airs of Scotland and India on their bagpipes. I had not been prepared for the evening chill, and before we were able to get back to our hotel I began to shiver uncontrollably. We were fortunate to be the recipients of the kindness of the British people who sat next to us because we discovered at the end of the performance there were no taxis available to enable us to get back to the hotel, and so they graciously went out of their way to see us to the hotel. It had not occurred to us to reserve a return taxi.

THE KHYBER PASS

On January 8, 2002, I happened to read in the BBC News, a special article by one of their correspondents, Matt Frei, which was entitled "Time Stands Still at Khyber Pass." The article begins at a military post at the Pass where Mr. Frei had just been given a luncheon by the officers. One of his hosts told him the story of a tree tied down with heavy chains. It seems a drunken British officer thought the tree was moving.

The tribal belt was set up after partition from India. It stretches for hundreds of miles along the border with Afghanistan, and although strictly part of Pakistan, it has its own laws and customs which no government is foolish enough to mess with.

Even under the Raj, the tribes were left to themselves. On the few occasions when contact was made, the regiment would dispatch a Political Agent.

In 1897, Major Sir Warburton (no other name) ventured into the Tira Valley, eighty miles from the Khyber Pass. This venture ended in disaster, and for 104 years the Tira Valley was not visited by any British or foreign army officer. The Khyber Rifles dispatched a helicopter and a platoon of men with a mule train. They set up a school and hospital and brought the first modern doctor these tribes had ever seen. The foregoing information acquired so belatedly may make my account of my visit to the Khyber Pass a bit more interesting.

We had reservations at the Shepherd Hotel in Peshawar because we planned to drive up to the Khyber Pass at the border between Pakhtunistan and Afghanistan. So the next day we flew from Lahore to Peshawar, over a dry, bony-looking country. Peshawar was a fascinating place–full of Pathans, who are a quite different sort of people from the Bengalis and the West Pakistanis.

I had seen a good many Pathans in Dacca because they came there to work as watchmen. Many of them are over six feet tall and some have blue eyes; possibly these are descendants from the soldiers of Alexander the Great's army.

At the hotel we negotiated for a car and driver to take us up to the Khyber Pass and back again. As usual in that part of the world, the amount of gas put into the tank is calculated to the last teaspoon, and if I had only known this at that time I would have gladly paid for an extra gallon or so. One learns by doing, however.

We made an early morning start. When we arrived at the checkpoint at the border between West Pakistan and the Pathan country, we were warned by the guards that we must be back across the border by four o'clock, since they would not guarantee our safety after that time, in accordance with an agreement with the Pakhtunistanis.

Setting out across more dry country, as we got further in we began to see what looked like fortresses--square mud-walled structures which could obviously accommodate a whole clan.

They were spaced quite far apart. In front of the gate was a sort of barrier which resembled the Chinese devil gate to keep evil spirits out. In this country however, it was done so no one could shoot straight into the courtyard. The countryside was brown, except that here and there we would see an apricot or almond tree in full glory of blossom.

The road climbed gradually. By the roadside we would see men and boys, each one carrying a rifle, with a bandolier of ammunition. No women were in sight except for one very surreptitious looking woman in rags, who had an apron full of sticks she was collecting in a gully.

As the land became hillier and steeper, we began to see the mouths of the cave-dwellings, which our driver pointed out to us. Apparently whole families live their entire lives in caves in Afghanistan. I made a jocose remark about probably the caves had wall-to-wall fleas, at which my American companion rightly reprimanded me for my insensitivity.

Near the pass we drove through a village which was famous for manufacture of arms, and again, there were lots of men about, but no women. We finally reached the pass, where there was a guard checkpoint, and were able to look across at Afghanistan, a wild and empty land. After that, there was nothing to do but turn back for Pakistan and our hotel. I read later that Alexander did not use the Khyber, but chose another pass farther south.

We were still in good time to make it back across the border, but I scolded the driver for putting the car in neutral in order to coast back down the hills from the pass. This is done customarily in order to save gasoline. I made him keep the car in gear because I didn't trust his brakes, which was a big mistake because we ran out of gas about fifteen miles from the Pakistan border. I learned to be sure and check, thereafter, that the driver had enough fuel to insure a safe return.

So there we were, stranded, and the sun was sinking lower all the time. The driver caught a ride on a passing truck to go buy some gas, and we sat and awaited our fate. A number of vehicles passed but we did not dare flag any of them down. Finally, when it was almost dark, a van with several Hindu gentlemen stopped to inquire if they could help. Blessings on their gentle Hindu hearts–they took us back to the hotel with no reproaches for our foolishness.

The next morning I had a big argument with the driver of the car, who actually expected to be paid the full amount we had agreed upon. I pointed out that he had not lived up to the bargain and refused to pay him the full amount.

In later years thinking over what might have happened to us in that wild and inhospitable place I finally began to realize what a lucky person I have been most of my life. Not always, but a lot of the time, especially when transiting Bulgaria on a train on the Orient Express, another experience I will write about.

I should mention here that East Pakistan, now called Bangladesh, is the delta of two enormous rivers, the Ganges and the Brahmaputra. The whole country is at sea level and is subject to severe flooding every year during the monsoon rains. It also is a very fertile rice-growing area and could be the "bread-basket" of that part of the world if properly managed.

I found it depressing to have no glimpse of sea or mountain when we lived in East Pakistan–the country was completely flat. I remember a great sense of euphoria which came over me the first time we flew into Katmandu for a holiday. Being in those awe-inspiring mountains was a lift to my spirits. And the Nepali people were so different from the Bengalis. The poverty was as bad, but they were all so cheerful. Perhaps the difference in the religion also made a difference, since the Nepalese are a mix of Buddhist and Hindu. Therefore the women are in evidence everywhere, not confined to their homes as the Muslim women are. I remember the cheerful country people coming in to the markets with huge cauliflowers as big as a bucket slung on each side of a carrying yoke.

'TIGER TOPS'

On our first visit to Nepal we went down from Katmandu and stayed at Tiger Tops for a week. Tiger Tops was down in the terai, or jungle area of Nepal, much lower in elevation than Katmandu. We flew there in a little DC3 with canvas sling seats, stopping at Pokhara to let off a Nepali woman who had a huge backpack. The pilot told us she would have to walk for a week through the mountains before she got home to her village.

Tiger Tops was named after the famous Tree Tops in Africa, and the sleeping rooms were up in the tops of enormous trees. The main meeting-dining room was down at ground level, but everything else was up in the trees.

Our little plane landed on a grass strip and then we had to be ferried across a river in a flat bottomed sort of country skiff, past gharials dozing on the mud flats. From there we went by jeep to Tiger Tops, not a great distance.

The area is a national park[1] reserve dedicated to preserving the beautiful tigers, small rhinos, and other wonderful jungle creatures. The park guards were Gurkhas who were all armed and had orders to shoot rhino poachers. There was–in fact, still is–a black market in rhino horns, as in the Orient they are believed to have aphrodisiac powers. The Gurkhas also had orders to protect us newcomers, and the manager of the place told us that for safety's sake we were never to venture away from the camp by ourselves without taking an armed guard.

As a matter of fact, we did see a marvelous leopard one afternoon when we were going somewhere in a jeep with the customary Gurkha-with-rifle perched in the back. All of a sudden, the driver stopped the jeep and pointed, and I could feel the tension in the Gurkha seated just behind us. Just a very short distance away, in the middle of the road we saw a magnificent leopard, who just stood there and stared at us for a lifetime, until finally he just de-materialized into the jungle. We were told that leopards are notoriously unpredictable in their mode of attack.

The first night at dinner, the manager informed us that a buffalo calf had been staked out as bait so we could go and see a tiger at his kill. I immediately protested that I did not want to have a calf sacrificed just so we could see a tiger. But the manager just said it was already "laid on," and a watchman would notify us when the kill had occurred.

Shortly before dinner was over word came that the kill had been made, and so we filed out: myself, Harold, a Portuguese lady doctor, and a Gurkha-with-rifle, and the driver. We bumped along a dirt road for a mile or so, and I was amazed to see dozens of bunny rabbits hopping in the headlights–I would have thought they would all have been eaten by the predatory animals.

When we got to where the kill was, we quietly got out of the jeep and with flashlights in otherwise complete darkness, we stumbled up the trail, falling over roots and other unseen objects. We arrived at a log shelter built around the trunk of a huge tree from which we could look down into a gully where the body of the calf lay. The driver shone a floodlight down to illuminate the area. Of course, having made all the noise we did, the tiger was alerted, and all we saw of him was his tail going quietly off-stage.

We waited half an hour but he did not come back so we finally gave up and started back in darkness for the jeep, being uncomfortably aware that somewhere not too far away was a tiger who had not finished his dinner.

We were somewhat disturbed at being forbidden to go and explore on our own, and especially so when, on a couple of our drives, we saw women out gathering firewood, completely unguarded by Gurkha-with-rifle. We would have enjoyed being able to go out and see the fantastic bird life that teemed in the jungle–peacocks were festooned up in trees, and there were parrots and other indescribably beautiful birds. But, on the other hand, we heard the coughing roar of the tigers at sundown, and perhaps the G-w-R escort was not such a bad idea.

A trip on an elephant was laid on for us, and that was an unforgettable experience. The object of the ride was to try to spot a rhino. We mounted from a platform halfway down the stair from our tree-top sleeping quarters. Hal and I sat in a little sort of platform with a low railing, lashed on the elephant's back, and the mahout sat in his customary place on the elephant's neck.

We descended a bank and crossed a shallow stream and started off into the jungle, hoping to encounter a rhino. These are a small variety of rhino, different from the ones in Africa, and are very wary of people and hard to see. The G-w-R informed us that the elephants are a bit afraid of the rhinos and would tremble if they got too close to one.

Having been a rider of horses it was quite interesting to notice how different the gait of an elephant is. One is rolled around by the one-foot-at-a-time gait, but once you get used to it, it is comfortable enough, and I imagine that where the mahout sits on the elephant's neck, the gait must feel rather different.

We arrived at an open space where there was grass as tall as the elephant's eye, and there was a sudden rustling sound, and the Gurkhas told us that it was a rhino. And yes, the elephant did tremble. But we never heard snort nor saw hair of any rhino.

My stay at Tiger Tops was blemished by a verbal exchange between Harold and the manager. In retrospect it can be put down to machismo, but the manager had been witness to an incident in Katmandu in which Harold had been very arrogant to a server in a hotel, and he brought this up in the argument which occurred at Tiger Tops. I felt extremely humiliated to be part of this, and later, when we stopped off at Pokhara on our return from Tiger Tops, I brought it up, and warned that I did not care to be a part of any more such incidents.

He knew I meant it–possibly remembering a similar incident that almost ended our marriage in its first year when one day he used a certain domineering, nasty tone of voice to me. I had immediately told him that if I ever heard that tone of voice again, I would be gone and wouldn't be coming back. Luckily for our marriage, he'd listened and remembered.

We arranged to stay overnight at Pokhara because I wanted to see the sunrise on Dhaulagiri and the other peaks. Annapurna was not far off, but I have forgotten the other names. We spent the night on cots in a small structure built entirely of corrugated iron, and it was so cold that it was impossible to sleep, but the discomfort was forgotten when the morning sun turned the peaks to rose and gold.

Some people have always been spiritually attracted to mountains, and I certainly found the Himalayas awe-inspiring. Why should anyone be awed by an aggregation of minerals which were upthrust by a convulsion of the earth's crust? Yet both Hindus and Buddhists have their holy places in the Himalayas, and the sight of Kanchenjunga, which we were granted just briefly one sunrise when it rose impossibly high above the clouds, brought me to tears.

KALIMPONG and DARJEELING

We were granted that brief glimpse of Kanchenjunga when we were staying at Darjeeling on a previous holiday journey from Dacca. On this trip we flew to a small town, name forgotten, where the famed mini-train started its journey up to Darjeeling. However, we made the tortuous journey by rented car with a driver. Our stay at the small hotel was enjoyable, and people who don't go to Darjeeling will never know what real Darjeeling tea tastes like.

While at Darjeeling we were able to make a journey to a cultural festival held at a place called Kalimpong, just fifteen miles from the border of Tibet. It was an exhausting but fascinating day. This is where we witnessed wonderful Tibetan dances performed by masked monks, and archery contests.

We also visited the Sherpa base in Darjeeling where Sir Edmund Hillary started his Everest climb. I have read that the way up Mount Everest is cluttered these days with rubbish left by climbers. I am very glad that the Nepalese government has made Kanchenjunga, their particularly sacred mountain, off limits to climbers.

On the way down from Darjeeling I began to feel unwell, probably from dust breathed in on our journey to Kalimpong, and by the time we reached Calcutta I had a very high fever, caused by one of the innumerable germs which infest that subcontinent. Luckily I had previously made an appointment to have a "curettage" at the only recommended hospital in Calcutta, and so was able to be admitted. I was kept abed for two weeks until I was well enough to have the curettage performed. Hal, of course, had to leave me to go back to work in Dacca.

When the day came for me to return to Dacca, I took a taxi to the airport. The airport officials saw that my permission to stay in India had expired by more than a week, so they told me I would have to go back to Calcutta and get the permit renewed before I could leave. At that moment I became so infuriated that I must have looked ten feet tall, and I absolutely refused to consider such a thing. I was not about to get involved in Calcutta bureaucracy. The officials wilted and stamped my ticket. (I am sure that my `aumakua* spirits were guarding me, the same as they did when I had that encounter in Bulgaria when I could have been thrown in jail. More of that later.)

When I arrived home again, to my sorrow I found that our beautiful Siamese cat had transferred his affections to our bearer and would not even look at me. He had been given to me as a kitten when Hal was trying to soothe my culture shock. We had been inseparable from the first moment, and it was hard for me to accept that he no longer wanted anything to do with me. *Inshallah!* (God willing!)

Incidentally, because of his beautiful blue eyes I had wanted to name him Maka, the Hawaiian word for eye. But Mr. Sheikh, the dredge base mechanical superintendent, who occasionally visited us, was horrified when I told him my choice of name and absolutely forbade me to use it. He said it would be a great insult to Islam to name a cat for their holy place, Mecca.[2] I explained that I thought the Hawaiian word was pronounced differently, but he would not hear of that name being used because the sound was too close.

LETTER from DACCA[1]

Home again in Dacca! After a month in India, and not at all strangely, the comfort we have made for ourselves here in this house (with the addition of our own rugs and pictures) seems very pleasant to relax into after all the experiences and vicissitudes of the last month. The few things that we have collected still have their charm, and this morning at 6:30 we sat on our lanai at our wicker breakfast table, eating a delicious papaya grown from the seeds I brought from Hawai`i.

Whether East Pakistan ever knows it, I think I have done them a great favor in introducing the solo papaya here into our garden. It will never be a compensation for all the unkind thoughts I entertain about the country, but let this at least be to my credit. (And after all, the opinion of this untutored person about the country may reveal more about the person than the country.)

At last another milestone has been passed in my life. Living in Dacca in the great flood plain of the Ganges and Brahmaputra Rivers, I felt hemmed in, with never a glimpse of sea or mountain, so pervasive in our life in Hawai`i. Ever since, as a girl of twelve or fourteen, when I read Kipling's *Kim* for the first time, I have had an emotional feeling about the Himalayas.

When on the first morning of arrival at Darjeeling we quite early toiled up the hill behind the hotel and saw holy Kanchenjungha, and the whole magnificent complex of snow peaks rising above the cloud-filled valley and foothills, I burst into tears at seeing such magnificence. It was a good thing I had my cry, because only once again did we get a glimpse of Kanchenjungha, and then there were just the very tips revealed, floating impossibly high in the air with masses of cloud swirling about them.

The rest of the time we had delightfully cold weather, with constantly rising and swirling clouds to temper the bright sunlight and clear air, but no peaks.

John Masters[2] says *Kim* is the best book ever written about India and I have re-read it here again, and I agree. So much has changed--the departure of the British Raj, the partition of India and Pakistan, yet some things are eternally India.

It is a long, wearying but beautiful drive from the plains to Darjeeling. It took us from noontime at Bagdogra till after dark to arrive at our hotel, in a very dilapidated old beige station wagon. Hal kept sneering at our driver, a weatherbeaten person who could have been Tibetan, or whatever race has the most mechanical aptitude, but to give credit where it is due, he tinkered and fussed and coaxed that old pile of scrap and bolts up to the top of the hill where Darjeeling stands, and never uttered one Tibetan cussword the whole time. Every time after the car gasped and died, he would climb out, fuss and tinker, then say "Tika" (Okay), and onward and upward we went.

On the way up we saw tiny kahili ginger growing, perhaps the ancestors of the ones which grow in Hawai`i.

After all our months spent in the flat lands of East Pakistan, our muscles and lungs required much painful adjustment, but after many persistent efforts, we were able to walk without toiling any more than could be expected. Our best effort was about a ten or twelve mile walk to the top of Tiger Hill where it is alleged a perfect view of both the Everest and Kanchenjungha complexes could be obtained, but it was not vouchsafed to us.

The people of that place are very interesting. Many, many Tibetans, of all degrees and clans, the sorriest of all being the destitute beggars who infested the approaches to the hotel, but ever so often could be seen a prosperous man or woman in their very handsome and distinctive garb. The manager of our hotel and his wife were well educated in India and America. Mr. Tenderflower (really, and truly, he uses this translation of his Tibetan name) resembles a taller version of a cultivated gentleman of Japan. His handsome son had been educated at Harvard and is a business man in India.

For the rest, since it was the time of Durga Puja,[3] there were a great many Hindus, who had come to the mountains to renew their mystic faith, the whole contributing to probably a more festive air than is customary. Buddhism is quite prevalent, but at the top of the hill where we got our first glimpse of the snow peaks are both Buddhist and Hindu shrines, and all day every day there were many people of both religions toiling upward to make their offerings.

Darjeeling in the old days of the British Raj was geared to the social life of the British, and so there are miles and miles of well-laid out walks and bridle paths, rather indifferently maintained these days, but still pleasant to walk on. Darjeeling is on a hogback at about 6,000 foot elevation, falling away steeply to valleys where ice-cold (but polluted) rivers wind their picturesque way, and beyond, about forty miles away, rising above ever bluer and steeper hills, are the eternal snows.

The little town and its bazaars teem with many races and there are little houses perched everywhere on the hillsides, so that nowhere can you escape the taint of human ordure and wood smoke on the air, which should be pure, but is not. And all the little sparkling watercourses tumbling down the hills are actually the drains of the houses above, but the people are cheery and strong and--heavens above!--how they can walk, swinging magnificently from the hip, up and down their steep hillsides, carrying burdens on their backs by a tote rope around their foreheads--men, women and children, all with burdens impossible to our eyes.

We spent an hour or so at the Himalayan Mountain Institute where the Sherpa Tensing Norgay now presides, and there is offered the bargain of bargains, if only we were young again: thirty-five days of basic mountaineering training, completely fed, clothed and housed, or rather tented, for only four hundred rupees. We also walked down to the Tibetan Self Help Refugee Centre where about sixty-five craftsmen and women live and turn out very handsome rugs in Tibetan and Chinese patterns, exquisite wood carvings, rather crude brass and copper work, and several other interesting articles for sale.

Two weeks in Darjeeling was rather enough, as after we covered all the paths within walking distance we felt a bit bored with our immediate surroundings, but the roads to anywhere at all are so terrifying that we did not venture anywhere else by car except for a one-day excursion to Kalimpong, only fifteen miles from the Tibetan border and thirty-five miles from Darjeeling. On that day a special tourist festival of Tibetan dances was being offered, and it was very well done, with fabulous brocade costumes and masks, and an archery contest afterwards with men wearing the most beautiful hand-woven, kimono-like robes, hitched up around knee level. The material was beautiful, hand-loomed cotton or wool, very heavy and in stunning colors of brown, ochre and madder and black.

However, it was too long a day for us and we had an altercation with the taxi service before we finally got started back to Darjeeling, with the result that it was dark when we started back over one hell of a dangerous road. We had refused to allow the driver to cram two more people in the back of our jeep, since there were already four of us there and three, including the driver, in the front seat. In several places there were complete corkscrew turns where the road climbed up out of the valley of the Teesta River. By the time we got back to the hotel our skins were black with germ-laden dust that contained something that laid me low for several weeks.

At 9:30 on the morning we left Darjeeling, I felt rather tired, still, I thought, from our excursion to Kalimpong, but by the time we reached Bagdogra airport in the plains I had a fever and a full-fledged case of influenza. Just by the happiest coincidence, I had previously arranged to enter Calcutta's one really good private nursing home for a three-day check-over and was scheduled to arrive on the night of our return from Darjeeling. So I had a hospital bed and excellent care, once I got there, and Hal left me there and went back to Dacca the next day, leaving me to recover at the hospital. After nine days of swallowing terramycin and vitamins, the doctors thought it safe to proceed with the original purpose of my visit and after that was over, I emerged into the smog of Calcutta.

There had been one very bad day in the hospital, when I felt strong enough one morning to totter out of bed and see who was wailing out on the very neatly paved and landscaped street in front of the hospital. There were the most appalling trio of a half-naked child (perhaps rented or stolen--such things happened in that country), a dwarfed, grimy, hunchbacked woman with her naked deformed back on display, and a spider-like crippled man creeping along on his bottom. They were addressing their pleas on this very clean and civilized street to the blank and sterile walls of the hospital. Filthy rags and matted hair completed the picture. Only the night before in one of my lucid moments I had again succumbed to that feeling of guilt about being so rich in the midst of so much poverty, and being able to lie in a private hospital room while the poor of Calcutta lie in the streets and when they die are taken away by the rubbish wagon.

I began to weep, and when the nurses finally called the doctor in, he asked me how long I had been in India. I was able to stop crying long enough to tell him I'd never live here long enough to become hardened to such sights. He attempted to comfort me by assuring me that this particular trio were professionals who spurned any efforts to help them as they made more money in their present condition. But this was no comfort to me because I have eyes to see and I have seen enough of this place to know they can't all be professionals.

But the sad fact is that one becomes calloused, as I am most of the time now. But never completely. Now I despise a country that forces one to be so inhumane.

As I have said before, I am so stinking filthy rich that while in Calcutta (during another visit) I bought a beautiful amethyst ring that goes from knuckle to first finger joint, and a topaz ring about the size of an ice cube--outrageously and ridiculously too big, but when I saw that glowing, golden sunset stone, I wanted it and no other. Plus topaz earrings to match! Jewelry such as mine is sneered at by Indian women because the stones are set in a gold alloy, whereas they insist on 24-carat, pure gold for the setting of their stones. After all, their jewelry constitutes the only security they can possess. By American standards, jewelry in Calcutta is a give-away.

In other shopping visits to Calcutta (when I bought the jewelry), there were fruits and vegetables to buy in the bazaars such as were never seen in Dacca. There were apples from Kashmir, walnuts from Dehra Dun, and bacon! The latter was unavailable in Muslim East Pakistan, and as a matter of fact, women, native and foreign, did not visit the markets in Dacca. Marketing in Dacca is a strictly male prerogative.

After the hospital stay I was anxious to return to Dacca, and so although the plane wasn't due to leave until 6:30 PM, I taxied out to the airport about four o'clock and sat there with a paperback, until time to depart. Finally I got my baskets and suitcase through customs and went to get my exit visa signed by the Immigration Officer, who said, "Where is your police permit to remain in India over 30 days?" It transpired that I had overstayed my leave while in the hospital. The airline official who might have prewarned me but didn't, calmly asked for my baggage checks so he could offload me so I could stay over and get the proper permission from God knows how many bureaucrats to leave Calcutta in who knows how many days? I was well accustomed to the "Come back Tuesday" statement made in every office in the Indian sub-continent. On hearing this official I became a Tall Tower of Cold and Quivering Rage and gave the poor little man cause to think I might, who knows, be Someone of Importance.   After scratching his head and sending desperate, fruitless messages into space, he allowed as how if I would write out a letter testifying that I was a Victim of Circumstances and asking for permission to leave India, I might be permitted to depart.   But it was lucky that I had that wad of receipted hospital bills in my bag as proof, in case my personality had not quite overwhelmed him. Didn't even have to cry, though I had that in reserve.

I think that the fact of my being able to keep my rage under control had something to do with the success of the affair, since a common vignette of Bengal, both in India and Pakistan, is two grown men standing nose to nose trying to outshout each other.

I can understand how India can have its fascination, especially for people who come from a cold climate where there seems to be so much more drabness. There is a tremendous sweep and diversity of warmth and color and vegetation and terrain, that to some might balance the cruelty and squalor and poverty. There is much to be learned here that I will never know.

***

FURLOUGH at HOME in HAWAI`I

When the time came for a break, we returned to Hawai`i. We had hoped to visit Sri Lanka, but were unable to arrange passage on a ship, from Chittagong, so instead, we flew to Bangkok, stopping briefly on the runway at Rangoon. Burma was locked up even more tightly at that time and we were not permitted off the plane.

Flying over Thailand on the way to Bangkok, I was impressed by the neatness of the landscape beneath us, with regularly shaped fields and good looking roads, and thought, at last we are returning to civilization, after the disorderliness of the Bengali landscape.

And indeed, although the Bangkok traffic in those days was nothing to what I understand it now is, it was by comparison to Dacca quite civilized. We stayed in a nice little hotel run by French people, and had dinner one evening at the famed Oriental Hotel, where I tasted a mangosteen for the first time. An indescribably wonderful flavor. It was presented in half-shell, with the little segments ready to be picked out with a small fork.

We cruised the *klongs*, or canals, and gaped at the glittering golden temples. I got so thoroughly relaxed in the lap of "civilization" that I ordered and ate a tossed green salad. Not the thing to do: I woke up in the middle of the night streaming from both ends and really thought I might not survive the night. After two careful years in Dacca, where I seldom had any problems because I strictly supervised the kitchen, I learned what "Delhi belly" was all about.

I recovered from the active emissions enough to get on a plane for Hong Kong, and arriving there, retired to the hotel room to continue recuperation. I ordered chook (rice soup), which had to be made specially for me, but it helped to restore internal comfort.

From Hong Kong we took a plane to New Zealand, arriving there in the beginning of the fall season, just the reverse of the other side of the equator. The poplar trees had turned golden, the air was cool and clean and refreshing, and we rented a car and drove for hundreds of miles. We were used to driving on the "wrong" side of the road, since we had driven in Pakistan, which had also inherited its driving style from the English.

After our years in East Pakistan, New Zealand was the perfect antidote. After being without fresh fruit of any kind except, of course, bananas, which could be peeled, our eyes lit on gorgeous piles of apples along the roadsides. Those days, the honor system prevailed, and next to the apples was a can with a slit in the top to put your money in. I wonder how it is there now. We left a trail of apple cores behind us wherever we went.

When we finally got home to Hawai'i and deplaned at the Honolulu airport, I was so glad to be home that I burst into great bawling sobs, but I didn't care. I had experienced many new and wonderful things, but in the mornings in Dacca when I awoke, I would lie there and think, "I can go home to Hawai'i."

When Hal would indulge in criticism of some aspect of life in Dacca, I would remind him, "It's their country." And I respected their feelings about their country. But, as a woman, I would never choose to live in a Muslim country. It was an eye-opener to me.

ALOHA `OE on the ORIENT EXPRESS

Life in Hawai`i was resumed with ease. I was welcomed back to the Bishop Museum Planetarium, and enjoyed working there and being at the Bishop Museum.

Our plans to return to East Pakistan were arrested by the Indo-Pakistani War of 1965,[1] which eventually led to the war between East and West Pakistan,[2] resulting in the creation of Bangladesh in what was formerly East Pakistan.

The Bengalis had always chafed under the assumption of superiority made by the West Pakistanis. I believe in spite of their all being the children of Allah, there was a color prejudice on the West side against the darker-skinned Bengali people, and the Bengalis insisted on political equality, building a "second capital" in Dacca.

Finally, after a year, Hal was approached by the Water and Power Development Agency to return to his former work at Narayanganj, in what was now Bangladesh, and we agreed that we would go for one more year. As before, Hal left ahead of me, and I stayed behind to finalize preparations for my departure. By then, Doug was married and Stephanie was working at the State Department in Foggy Bottom, in Washington.

I planned my 1967 trip to Dacca with a stop in Washington to visit Stephanie. It was a beautiful springtime there, full of blossoming trees and shrubs, especially the dogwoods and azaleas.

I had learned that a major horse show was scheduled in England, so from Washington my route took me to London, where a very agreeable tourist organization called HOTAC (Hotel Accommodations) International helped me find a hotel near Windsor, where the horseshow was to be held. The show was held at the foot of Windsor Castle on a wide grassy plain, and was a revelation to me of British spit and polish. The horses were groomed to perfection, and as each rider mounted, an aide would rush up with a cloth and whisk any speck of dust off the boots. There were all sorts of exciting events, and there were driving competitions in which the Duke[3] took part. Beer companies entered enormous drays drawn by matched teams of huge Clydesdales. And there was an entry of almost a hundred Arab horses in a halter class. There was one fiery chestnut with flowing mane and tail, which kept my eye, and sure enough, he won first place.

On the last daytime performance, the Queen's Household Guard performed a special exercise in honor of the Emir Faisal, from Saudi Arabia, who happened to be visiting the Queen (Elizabeth II). It was a brilliantly executed drill of pairs of horses pulling small cannons, one horse of the pair being ridden by an officer, and accompanied by another mounted officer. The whole thing was performed at a breakneck gallop around an arena, with crisscross figure-eight movements performed with split-second precision. It took my breath away and I was on the edge of my chair during the entire time. I was fortunate to have been able to witness such a once-in-a-lifetime spectacle.

By the way, for a guinea (I think about $20 U.S.), I got admitted to the members' enclosure and sat with all the lords and ladies. I had explained that I was from Hawai`i and really wanted to see the fronts of the horses, since their rears were presented to the hoi-polloi in the bleachers. So the people in the admission kiosk, for a guinea, kindly let me in for the whole five days. I found the lords and ladies were very nice, although they must have wondered who the hell I was. I didn't fit into any familiar slot there, and in other places too, people wondered what country I came from.

The last evening was devoted to the presentation of prizes, given by Her Majesty, herself. At the end of the evening, the Queen and Duke got into a special limousine with glass and special illumination all around so everyone could see them. They were driven all around the field to greet everyone, and there were loud and heartfelt hurrahs, and "God-bless-the-Queen"-s. When reading of all the troubles of the Royals since then, I have wondered how much of that genuine love for their Royals survived the Queen's *annum horribilis*.

THE ORIENT EXPRESS

While still in Honolulu and planning my trip to join Hal in Dacca, I had decided that instead of just flying there and seeing little but clouds, I wanted to take the Orient Express as far as I could go on it. In Hawai`i train travel is non-existent, and I always had the desire to travel that way. So, after the horse show was over, I went back to London for a night or two.

I made a visit to the Planetarium in that city, and the wax museum which was nearby, and the British Museum. London seemed such a safe and friendly city that I did not mind being alone without a traveling companion. One day when I got into an elevator, there was an older Chinese couple in it. One look at them told me they were from Hawai`i, so we greeted each other. One of the games I played while traveling alone was to guess what nationality certain people might be. I think I was right most of the time. On the other hand, people everywhere could not seem to be able to figure out where I came from. They never thought I was an American.

Paddington Station was my departure point on the Orient Express. While I was waiting to board my train I was accosted by a young man who struck up a conversation with me, wanting to know where I came from. His manner was rather familiar and I was not about to strike up a friendship with a total stranger, so when I got on board I prudently chose a compartment with a very proper English lady sitting in it. The fellow went back and forth in the corridor peering in at us, but finally decided I was not worth the effort after all.

The Orient Express to Istanbul started from London and went across the English countryside to the ferry point on the coast. I believe it was Dover to Calais. The very pretty Kent countryside was interesting because there were a number of oast houses which my compartment companion told me were for drying hops.

The trip across the Channel was not as rough as I had expected. I remember that some people were seasick, and a lot of glassware in the bar fell down with a crash, so it probably was rough. I think I would prefer the channel to the new Chunnel, which gives me the horrors to think about. When we arrived at Calais in late afternoon, the train was waiting right there and I found my private compartment and settled in for the night after a visit to the dining car. The compartment had a comfortable seat which the porter made up into a berth at night. There was a little fold-down washbasin, and a luggage rack, and a nice window that opened, and it was my very own little private, rolling viewpoint of Europe.

The train route skirted the great city of Paris and I never saw a glimpse of it. I remember waking briefly at Lyon, and fell asleep again. The next thing I remember was the sound of cow bells, very melodious, and pushing up my compartment window, saw a herd of brown Swiss cows coming down the road. It was early morning and we were stopped at the Swiss border.

Crossing Switzerland, we started through the Simplon, that long, long tunnel under the Alps. The lights dimmed and it seemed to take forever, but finally we emerged in Italy. The route went South along Lake Maggiore, very beautiful, bypassing Milan, and eventually ending up at Venice.

EASTERN EUROPE (lower portion)

I had scheduled a couple of days in Venice, and in retrospect am sorry that I did not allow more time because it was such a fascinating and beautiful place. I remember sitting, alone as usual, in the great Piazza San Marco as the moon rose, and watching the people who came from all over the world to enjoy that marvelous place. Access to the Piazza from my hotel, which was just off the Grand Canal, was easily gained through a little side door in the hotel, and down an alley.

It was such a pleasure to be able to explore on foot with not a single automobile to sully the atmosphere. I missed out on my hoped-for gondola ride because time passed too rapidly, and had to rely instead on the sleek speed boats which served as water taxis.

There was a nice-looking American couple sitting next to my table in the hotel garden dining area, and since I was tired of being alone I invited them to join me for a drink. They were from New Hampshire and were a pleasure to be with. We agreed on an excursion the next day to a small island which had a fascinating history, with a Christian church built on the mosaic-floored foundation of a Roman temple. Through an arrangement made at Harry's Bar we were able to hire a speedboat to take us there, passing Murano, the island of the glass makers and stopping for lunch under a charming waterside pergola covered with grapevines.

The trip to Istanbul resumed with an evening spent passing the somewhat grimy industrial part of Trieste, and across Yugoslavia, arriving at Belgrade some time in the morning. When I think of the horrors of Bosnia which we have just witnessed, I find it difficult to reconcile them with my experience in Belgrade.

Belgrade was a change point for trains. From there trains went to Vienna, Istanbul, or Athens. In Venice I had changed some dollars to dinars, having been warned that there would be no dining car after Venice. There was a little railway station food shop so I, speaking nothing but English, went over and selected by pointing at a couple of rolls stuffed with what looked like ricotta, some oranges, and a big brown bottle of beer, because I had been warned about the drinking water from that point onward.

I then looked inquiringly at the vendor and fanned out the dinars so he could take what he wanted. A group of curious men had gathered around me, and a hand reached over my shoulder and selected the correct amount of money and put it down on the counter. Not a word was exchanged, only a grateful smile from me.

A porter had taken my bags over to the right platform for the Istanbul departure, so I bundled myself and my food on board and settled down again in my new compartment.

At the border of Bulgaria, I was asked to pay a ten-dollar fee for the privilege of transiting the country, although I was not going to set foot on it. I had not been warned about this by the Honolulu travel agent, and I stubbornly decided that I would play dumb and say that in spite of the American money tucked in my bra, I could not pay, offering them dinars instead, which they spurned, insisting on American money.

The border officials apparently gave up and did not insist, after they saw my papers from Hawai'i, but sometime late that night I heard a key in the lock of my compartment door. The door opened and there stood a uniformed man, shiny boots, Sam Browne belt, pistol and all, who gruffly barked *Pasaporte!* at me. The porter was standing behind him in the corridor and I gave him what we Hawaiians call "steenk-eye" as I fumbled for my passport. I had to surrender it and I spent the rest of the night wondering if I was going to end up in a Bulgarian jail. It was a case of the valor of ignorance, and sometimes I marvel at the luck of this innocent from Hawai'i, traveling alone all the way to Bangladesh, without getting into trouble.

We skirted the city of Sofia in the distance and eventually crossed the Turkish border at a place called Edirne. That part of the country was rolling grassland with scattered clumps of trees, and the train chugged along through that mostly empty landscape, with just a few peasant women here and there, wearing baggy Turkish bloomers and head scarves.

When I say "chugged" in relation to our progress, that is the correct word, and the word "express" did not mean speed. As we crossed borders there was always some time spent backing and filling onto side rails, and changing cars. Altogether a leisurely way to travel which I enjoyed. After all, the Orient Express by the time I traveled on it, was quite venerable and was not far from retirement. By comparison the crack Japanese passenger trains we experienced in Japan were quite speedy.

Arrival at the train station in Istanbul was confusing, but I got myself and my baggage through customs. That station was where I learned the value of traveling light. Hal had warned me that shoes were not of good quality in Dacca so I had packed an extra bag with shoes. While I was struggling with my extra luggage, all the taxi drivers were clamoring for my business. I picked a driver who had an antique Chevrolet and he loaded my bags in the trunk. When I got into the back seat he turned around in a rather belligerent way (perhaps the Islamic way of addressing strange women), and stated the price for the ride to the Intercontinental Hotel. I had done my homework and knew he was doubling his price and I got mad, said, "The hell with you Jack!" and got out of the taxi. I dickered with the surrounding men, arrived at the right price with one of them, and had my luggage transferred to his taxi. I arrived at the Intercontinental Hotel without further incident.

Turkey has always fascinated me because of its culture and history and my stay there was regrettably too short.

The next day was a state holiday and had something to do, I think I remember, with Atatürk, their revered premier who took the veils and fezzes off the citizens of Turkey. While I was in the hotel lobby sipping Turkish coffee a very frazzled looking young American woman came over and asked if she could join me at my table and I welcomed her. She was a creamy-skinned, buxom redhead, just the type men (especially Turks) drool over. She said she needed to shake off a man who had approached very closely behind her while she was out street-side watching the parade, and had an erection, rubbing himself up against her. She had fled into the hotel seeking sanctuary at my table because she was afraid he had followed her.

I learned from her that she was an art teacher who had been in Egypt and with all the other Americans had been ordered to leave the Middle East because of imminent danger of involvement in a crisis. I did not take what she said seriously as involving myself, and next day, with a female Magyar guide, toured Topkapi Palace and the Grand Bazaar, where I haggled for a rug and purchased one which I still enjoy. The Grand Bazaar needs much time to explore, but at least I got a taste of it.

Having enjoyed my Orient Express ride so much, I decided to go to a travel office and change my air ticket from Istanbul to Ankara to a rail ticket. I had been invited to spend a week in Ankara with Jim and Naomi Thomas, at that time stationed there for USAID.[4]

At the travel agency there was such a hubbub that I inquired as to the reason and was told that foreigners were desperately trying to get out of the Middle East.[5] Realizing that my onward journey to Dacca might be jeopardized, I phoned Naomi in Ankara and told her I thought I ought to skip my visit with them and continue directly to Karachi and on to Dacca. She objected that she had planned a dinner party around my arrival and so I agreed to spend a couple of nights with them and then cross the border by air, and to Beirut.

Changing my plans was a good idea, although I was sorry I did not have more time in Ankara–what a fascinating place it was. As it was, I at least visited the "Citadel," an ancient stronghold whose walls were studded with pieces of ancient marble columns and building materials from Greek and Roman times. Also, the Hittite museum was full of the most fascinating and surprising sculptures.

Leaving Ankara we touched down briefly in Beirut and again I had "time to kill," so I visited more rug bazaars for the fun of haggling, but did not buy anything.

ON to WEST PAKISTAN

I flew to Karachi next, where I was admitted into West Pakistan. I had a bottle of whiskey in my luggage which I had bought at a duty-free shop for Hal. The customs men wanted to take it away from me as alcohol is forbidden to Muslims, but I "put on my shawl" and said it was a gift to my American husband whom I had not seen for months. Being crotchety from my long flight, I was prepared to drop it right on the concrete floor, but was waved aside by the men and allowed to keep it.

So on to Dacca and a reunion with Hal, a skinny rack of bones, as usual, thanks to the dysentery. After a good night's sleep we woke up to the news the Six-Day War between Israel and Egypt had begun. *Whew!* Surely my `aumakua had been guiding me to keep moving.

Memories of our second stay in Dacca are fading. We had a different house with terazzo floors, again quite spacious, on the opposite side of Dhanmandi Lake. We were able to get our same bearer, Tony (a Christian), back again, and also the same *mali*. Time passed, and Hal was invited to prolong his work for another year and he was tempted to stay. But when he asked me how I felt about it, I looked him right in the eyes and asked him, "Do you want to die here?" And truly, he could have died because of the ever-present necessity of field trips which caused him to become ill from drinking unboiled water.

There had been conversations with other expatriates like ourselves, about what would happen in case of a death. Burial space was at a premium, and rumor had it that graves were routinely dug up and bones dumped in trash heaps. My own feeling was that if I were to die in that country, I would want to be dumped in the sacred Ganges.

Those enormous rivers made their own laws. During the monsoons the English language newspaper routinely carried articles about the erosion of some poor farmer's land. In many places they were so wide that the other side was barely visible.

Speaking of those rivers, I had an interesting experience on our first "tour of duty" in East Pakistan. We had a very active and enterprising young American couple as neighbors on the south side of our place. They had explored the Hill Tracts and gone many places which I had only heard of. They brought water-skiing equipment with them, and one day they invited me to accompany them on a water-skiing picnic about forty miles down-river from Dacca.

I accepted gladly and was invited to fly down with a Pakistani pilot named Rashid. He was from Lahore but came to East Pakistan every summer to teach flying to young army officers. He had a Grumman ski-plane which was a very neat, tight little aircraft. Rashid asked me if I minded if he took a student along to work on water landings and, of course, I agreed. When we got down to the area where our friends were to arrive with their speedboat, he began showing the student first of all how to make the approach run, and then how to land on the water. I will bet that I could have landed that plane myself by the time that episode was over after listening to Rashid's coaching and the tension in his voice. The young student badly flubbed the first few attempts and we sent up great plumes of water.

By that time our friends the Downings had arrived, with Pam, our friend of the Quaker Relief Station. Rashid ferried the student pilot back and returned to join us. We were all wearing bathing suits under our shirts and shorts, and the Downings started the waterskiing, while I, having never been very good at it, sat on the shore of the sandbar where we had planned to have our picnic lunch.

The sandbar was in the middle of a river which must have been a mile wide and the countryside appeared completely uninhabited. When we began to spread out our picnic, in a relatively short time men and boys paddling the local boats began to arrive. Of course the spectacular splashes made by the flying student's attempts at landing had attracted them, as well as the waterskiing itself.

Soon we were completely surrounded by a ring of men and boys, and their stares at us women in our bathing suits and their comments about us did not seem very nice to me.

Pakistani women might expose their bare midriffs when they wore saris but bare legs were never exposed. I uneasily covered myself as well as I could with my beach towel.

There were too many of them to invite them to participate in our picnic and I began to be really uneasy. Then one of the men asked for a cigarette and was given one by Rashid. Shortly thereafter one of the boys leaned down and picked up a package of cigarettes (American cigarettes were much coveted).

Just about then, Rashid said very quietly to us, "It is time for us to leave." We heard him, quickly picked up our belongings, and the Downings and Pam got in the boat. When Rashid and I went to board our plane the men were hanging on to the pontoons and Rashid said something very quietly to them, at which they relinquished their grasp and we were able to take off.

This episode was another confirmation of the extreme over-population of that country. It was quite impossible to go anywhere to commune with nature without being immediately joined by at least one curious person, but more like dozens of them. In the wide, lonely reaches of the Brahmaputra River there was no escape from humankind.

HOMEWARD BOUND from DACCA

W hen it became time for us to leave, our friends Shirley and Bob Bridges arranged an enormous farewell party for us with Hawaiian music, and leis, and pseudo-Hawaiian food (curry served in coconut shells). I am embarrassed to say that it all made me so homesick that I shed some tears.

The Bridges were wonderfully friendly folks and we enjoyed their company. After we left what was now Bangladesh–our final departure in the late 1960s–we rarely saw them, except for one very remarkable meeting which still causes me to ponder.

In the early 1990's, about fifteen years after we moved to Kaua`i, I took a friend up to see the Waimea Canyon, a famous visitor site. While I was standing at the railing I heard a woman right next to me saying to her companion, "Frances brought me here the last time I came to Kaua`i." I could only see her back and that of her companion, so I peered around and said, "Frances who?" And, of course, it was Bob and Shirley Bridges, newly arrived on Kaua`i–she from California to meet her husband, who had flown in from the Philippines.

On our departure from Dacca we arranged to fly to Penang in Malaysia, which was touted to us while we were in Dacca, as being like Hawai`i. It isn't.

Hal and I stayed at a hotel on a beach for a couple of days, and then took a Mercedes taxi down the Malay Peninsula, to Kuala Lumpur. That was a fascinating view of Malaysia, viewed at about a hundred miles an hour from the windows of the Mercedes. It included some strange geologic features–apparently limestone outcrops which thrust abruptly up out of the landscape, like gigantic cupcakes, sometimes with little temples nestled on them.

We spent one night at a hotel in Kuala Lumpur, and the next day took a rental car with driver and drove to Malacca, on the Strait of Malacca, across from Sumatra. We had been told of an exquisite little Chinese temple there, which we enjoyed visiting. There were fascinating remnants of the European and other cultures that had been there in ancient times.

From Kuala Lumpur we took a marvelous old-fashioned train to Singapore on a special car that had red plush revolving chairs and bar service. We reveled in such antique luxury.

`ekolu / three

PHOTO ALBUM

Capt. William Alfred Todd, Frances' maternal grandfather, in his official portrait as Fire Chief, County of Hilo, Hawai`i, Territory of Hawai`i.

Maternal grandfather of Frances Nelson Frazier.

*William Alfred Todd
Fire Chief · County of Hilo. Hawaii, T.H.*

Richard Nelson, Master Mariner and Ships' Captain; father of Frances Nelson Frazier.

Thought to have been taken in his thirties; professional portrait by Rice & Perkins, Honolulu, Hawai`i.

All photos from the author's photo albums except those marked otherwise.

(Above)" USS St. Mary's" (1843 - 1908), Naval Historical Foundation

(Below) The "Tillie E. Starbuck"-- Dyal Ships Collection

A view of Lanikai on the windward (east) shore of, O'ahu, Hawai'i, where the Nelson
family's modest beach home was located off by itself when the author and her brothers were
growing up and enjoying weekends and school vacations far from life in "town"–Honolulu.
(From a print in the author's collection made from Williams' 1926 negative, Hawai'i State
Archives)

A young Frances decked with multiple, fragrant plumeria lei in a Honolulu garden on a milestone occasion–maybe graduation.

Julian Nelson, Frances' younger brother, with bride Evelyn (Yap) Nelson on their wedding day.

Richard Nelson and Ellen Eva (Todd) Nelson, Frances' parents.

Taken in California during retirement years following July 1945, when they traveled the Mainland staying in trailer parks, enjoying the "gypsy life" that covered about 50,000 miles from Oct. 1939 to July 1941. Richard kept detailed travel notes, a large body now lost, some saved in his "Diary and Ships' Log."

Ellen's seasonal allergic skin reaction to mangoes often sent her away from Hawai'i to the Mainland U.S.A.

(Above) 1938 Buick pulling a Pierce Arrow trailer, one of the car-trailer rigs Frances' parents used to explore the Mainland.

(Left) Frances, the horsewoman, astride her "Anglo-Arab" horse, the last of many beloved horses she has ridden and owned.

On Kaua`i, she enjoyed riding with artist friend Jean Gregg, particularly the Kalaheo pasture-lands. ("No cars!")

Mother and Child: The author with Douglas, the Fraziers' son, taken looking seaward from the `Aiea Heights home property on O`ahu.

Frances and Hal's firstborn arrived in Nov. 1939, prior to the terrifying events of Pearl Harbor, when his mother protected him from strafing bullets after she watched the harbor area explode and burn, wondering if husband Hal were alive.

Outdoor playtime: Douglas (l.), "the dark one," and sister Stephanie, the Fraziers' "Boomer baby" (born Oct. 1942), and admittedly "the light one" of the two Frazier children.

(Above) Frances before the Academy Art Center, Honolulu, where she worked as volunteer social secretary for a time in the 1950s. (Photos courtesy Anita Manning)

(Below) Keahualaka, Ha`ena, Kaua`i–Hal smiles on while *hānai* daughter Anita Manning shares something the *ti*-leaf draped Frances finds very amusing.

Happy threesome: Frances, daughter Stephanie and Hal out for an evening in Po'ipu.

Taken before Hurricane 'Iniki devastated the island of Kaua'i (9-11-1992).

Koke'e cabin: Stephanie Frazier (l.) with parents, Frances and Hal Frazier, and their pet, little "Meali'ili'i."

Taken outside the late Peter Dease's cabin, the site of many enjoyable forest stays during a long friendship.

(Above) In the aftermath of `Iniki, the first `Oma`o home: roofless, wall-less and drenched. The Fraziers were safe, lived in their garage until the new home (r.)was completed–same site, on a slab, reinforced with hurricane ties–toward the end of 1993.

Frances and Hal with their pet German shepherd, rescued by Frances.

Stephanie and "Mom," the author, during an evening with writer friends in Wailua, Kaua'i, Oct. 2005, during the dedication to Frances (and Roselle F. K. Bailey) of the newly published *Behold Kaua'i, Modern Days ~ Ancient Ways.* (Photo by Dawn F. Kawahara)

(Below) Frances in Feb. 2004, when she was honored as a Kaua'i "Living Treasure" by the Kaua'i Museum in Lihu'e, here flanked by a display of her memorabilia– including a portrait of her young married self (wreathed in a ginger lei) and numerous awards for her translations.

`ehā / four

HAWAI`I *NEI*

1960s to Present

COURT CASES

While we lived in East Pakistan and then in Bangladesh, I had a small library of books in Hawaiian, such as Fornander's Hawaiian-English books, published as Bishop Museum Bulletins. I would cover up the page with the English translation and attempt to puzzle out the Hawaiian.

When we returned to Honolulu after our final stay in Bangladesh, a friend of mine who was a partner in a title guaranty company, knowing my interest in the Hawaiian language, asked me if I would like to try translating some Hawaiian land conveyance documents. Her translator had recently died and she needed a new translator. So I took some copies of Hawaiian deeds home and worked on them, and then sent them to Zelie Sherwood, a well-known translator who by then had retired to her home on Moloka`i, asking her if she would look them over and criticize them. I did not know Zelie personally but knew she been the State's translator.

She was kind enough to read my translations and wrote me back that I was on the right track and that she would be glad to help at any time. I have cherished that letter[1] for many years. This pursuit led to a new way of life in that I began to do translations for title companies and law firms and found it very interesting.

What a translator of legal documents must always keep in mind is that moment of truth when you may have to defend your translation in court. The necessity for truth and accuracy is very much on my mind whenever I have done this work. I have seldom in my translating lifetime been called to appear in court to defend a translation. The times when this did happen served as learning experiences, and I found myself able to hold my own with lawyers.

Fortunately, it has been necessary for me to make only four appearances in court. My first experience was in Honolulu, and at that time I was accepted in court as an expert witness. I really have no certificate of any kind because there was no means of achieving one. I simply started doing translations and became accepted as a translator. At the time I began this type of work, Hawaiian was considered a dead language and there were very few classes, and no specific class to teach the work I was doing. I developed my way of translating on my own, and it seems to be acceptable because many people and firms have asked for my work.

I had a strange experience once long ago when I was called to appear in court in Kona, Island of Hawai'i, on the case of a Hawaiian man who had previously been successful in stopping development plans for a luxury hotel in South Kohala, and had received a settlement sum. In this case in which I was called to appear on the side of the defendant, the plaintiff stated that he was connected in his genealogy to Queen Kalama (the wife of King Kalakaua) and therefore claimed ownership of a vast tract of her land near the little port of Kawaihae. He was unable to produce any legitimate documents. His sole evidence was a scrap of paper with a few unintelligible words scribbled on it, which he said had been found in the Queen's Hawaiian Bible. He claimed that this scrap of paper had been written on by the Queen. I could not make any sense of the words scribbled on the paper. His lawyer was quite ignorant of Hawaiian land terms and asked me a number of questions which I was able to answer quite simply. I was kept on the witness stand for over an hour, answering questions.

When I was able to be excused from court, after my testimony, I was hurrying from the courtroom to make a flight to Honolulu. A very handsome Chinese woman, whom I believe was the wife of the plaintiff, stood up, stopped me and embraced me and gushed, "You were simply wonderful!" To this day I cannot figure out why she said this when I had just shot her husband down with my testimony.

The third court appearance was in Hilo before a judge who apparently was impressed by me when I appeared before him in a case involving some land in North Kohala. That was the last time I ever appeared in court and I want to say that sitting on a hard wooden bench outside a courtroom, waiting to testify, sometimes for hours, even all day, is not my idea of the best way to spend my time.

A case which tickled me, however, was a case that never had to go to court. This case happened some time after my appearance in the Kona Courthouse. It was to be tried before Judge Kubota in Hilo. The State of Hawai'i was contesting the claim by (I think) a sugar company, about a parcel at the little landing called Māhukona, in Kohala. The State Attorney was suing the owner of the land for a reason which I do not remember. The reason I was involved was because of the land survey description of the area in which the State's surveyor took the word *honua* to mean land which was absolutely flat. I disagreed with this and planned, if I had to go to court, to take along my Hawaiian Bible, which "in the beginning" says: "*I kinohi hana ke Akua i ka lani me ka honua.*" In the Hawaiian Bible, *honua* is used for the earth in all its aspects, and since the earth is obviously not flat, but has many ups and downs, how could the surveyor translate *honua* as meaning flat? However, the night before I was scheduled to fly to Hilo to appear in court, the lawyer who had hired me phoned to say that the court case was off. The judge remembered me because about a year previously I had appeared in his court in a case concerning some land in North Kohala. He had scheduled a meeting between the State's surveyor and the lawyer for whom I was to appear. The lawyer told me that at the meeting, the judge said to the Surveyor, "You want to have Mrs. Frazier fly all the way down to Hilo from Kaua`i to answer this question? You will be wasting your time; you'll never shake her." So the case was settled, and I never had the chance to brandish the Hawaiian Bible in court. Actually, I was rather disappointed because I did not get the chance to show off, and that's probably a very good thing.

As I write this a case on Maui is pending, in which I may have to appear. I again plan, if called to court, to take the Hawaiian *Kauoha Hou*, the New Testament, as my reference. Again, the State Surveyor is involved (though not the same one). A couple had purchased some parcels of land on Maui. These parcels were originally sold by the Commissioners to Quiet Land Titles and the surveys of the parcels appear in the Land Commission Award as well as in the Royal Patent granted on this award. In the survey of one of the parcels, one course ran along the sea, described by the Hawaiian term "*e pili ana i ke kai,*" meaning "along the sea." The Hawai`i State land map, however, showed the parcel as being inland, away from the seashore.

The land owners paid a surveyor to make an independent survey, which confirmed my translation. The owners have sued the State of Hawai`i. The Defendant, Attorney General Earl Anzai (who lost his position in the Republican election triumph), averred in his response to the Plaintiffs that: "the property description written in the Hawaiian language in the Royal Patent and translated for Plaintiffs by Francis [sic] N. Frazier, can have more than one translation in English." This attorney general has now been supplanted by a new Republican attorney general, and so I am disappointed that I will not have the opportunity to face my accuser in court.

I have been gleefully hoping for the opportunity to stand up in court and respond: "Yes, indeed, the attorney general is correct that the phrase *"e pili ana i ka kai"* can have more than one meaning in English. For instance, *kai* can also mean "soup" or "gravy." So it would be quite possible to translate that course as, "North 82 1/40 West 9.70 chains along the gravy (or the soup)."

Then, just as I would have quoted from Genesis in the Hawaiian Bible to confirm the usage of the word *"honua,"* I would have taken a sentence from the New Testament in Mark IX:42, *"A o ka mea hoohihia mai i kekahi o ka poe liilii nana wau e manao io mai nei, e aho nona, ke nakinakiia ka pohaku wili palaoa ma kona ai, a e hooleiia ku ia iloko o ke kai."* ("And whosoever shall offend one of these little ones that believe in me, it is better for him that a millstone were hanged about his neck, and he were cast into the sea.")

My STINT at the HAWAI`I STATE ARCHIVES, HONOLULU

In July of 1973, when I became fifty-nine years old, I went back to work, the first time I had been a salaried employee since I left the Board of Water Supply years before, except for my little job at the Bishop Museum Planetarium in the late 1950s.

The Hawai`i State Archives advertised the position of Hawaiian Translator that year, and I noticed the ad in the newspaper but thought nothing of it. But Harold said, "That's a job you could handle. Why don't you go and apply for it?" I pooh-poohed the idea, but just for the heck of it showed up for the examination. Although I felt quite comfortable with my ability to translate the Hawaiian language into English, I have always considered myself a "book Hawaiian." In other words I am not a speaker from birth, and though I can converse in Hawaiian I am not as fluent as a native speaker. Therefore I did not feel I could qualify.

There were, I seem to remember, about seven applicants including myself. One of the questions in the examination had to do with a Hawaiian land survey, and it just happened that my engineer husband had familiarized me with the terms. I was quite familiar with the language in the deeds I had been translating for various clients since the encouragement I had received from Zelie Sherwood.

Apparently I must have been the only one who knew how to translate surveys and so, to my surprise I was hired. At that time the Archives was run by Agnes Conrad, a woman with an incredible knowledge of the history stored there, of which she was the custodian and guardian. Thus began another shift in my life which brought me many rewards. I remember walking through the palace grounds after the interview with Miss Conrad, and seeing a rainbow over the mountains – and I knew that this was an emblem especially for me.

When I went in for my first day at the Archives, a small building under an enormous banyan tree, I felt very awkward and unsure of myself. When Agnes took me to my new office, a very pleasant room with a view out into the Palace Grounds, I asked her where my typewriter was. She replied that no Hawaiian translator before me had ever used a typewriter. Their work was written out in longhand on yellow pads, after which her secretary typed them. I laughed when she showed me an antique Underwood typewriter which was so old it had hearts and flowers painted on it. She promised to order me an electric typewriter through DAGS, the Department of General Services. In the meantime I brought my portable typewriter from home.

I had a nice office from which I could see all the passers-by, and in season, on the patch of lawn outside my window there would be a plover. I could watch it while mulling over the translation I was doing, which took me back to the year 1845. This was the beginning of a job which took three years to complete and with which I became totally obsessed. I did it all on my little portable typewriter and the joke is that on the day that I told Agnes that I had decided to resign because I wanted to move to Kaua`i, she looked at me and said, "I'm not sure how to tell you this, but the order for your typewriter just came through!"

The work which kept me busy and obsessed was the translation of the Native Register of claims made by the Hawaiian people to the Board of Commissioners to Quiet Land Titles. This is not the place to enter into a historical dissertation about land in Hawai`i, but briefly: in 1845 American missionaries who had gained influence in the government of the Hawaiian Kingdom persuaded Kamehameha III that all the land in Hawai`i ought to be divided up. This radical change in land ownership is called the Mahele, or the Great Mahele.

A very brief explanation is probably in order here, since that period of Hawaiian history is still not very well known except to historians. During and previous to the reign of King Kamehameha III, no one owned land in the Hawaiian islands, not even the *ali`i*, or chiefs. The land was the province of numerous gods, and the *ali'i* had stewardship, but not ownership. By the time of Kamehameha III, foreigners, especially American missionaries, had gained influence over the King, and he was persuaded that in order to join the civilized nations the land of Hawai`i should be divided up into the crown lands, the lands of the nobles, or *ali'i,* and land for the support of the government. Then someone thought of the common people, the *maka`āinana*, and so claimants were allowed to present their claims for lands which they had occupied and improved.

These claims were preserved in the Native Register, which I translated in its entirety. The original folio volumes had been photocopied (very badly) and I was furnished with very old and discolored photostats, two for each page because of the folio size of the volumes. Fortunately the handwriting on the pages was generally quite beautiful, although sometimes difficult to read because of the discoloration of the paper. There were eleven volumes, starting with the land at the then Honolulu waterfront, and ending with claims made on the island of Kaua`i. They were all in the Hawaiian language and many of them were quite rudimentary and naive, and I found the claims quite fascinating and endearing. There were only 11,309 claims, and not all of the claimants received Royal Patents if they received Land Commission Awards. Those claims were recorded in the Native Register.

There were so many fascinating little items that yet remain clear in my mind. For instance, in one survey of a piece of property, the description said, "Go North six *anana* (fathoms), then around Mr. Jarvis's bathhouse. . ." This particular Jarvis was an early newspaperman and historian, and his bathhouse was long gone.

Occasionally a claimant would illustrate his claim with a sketch of a grass house and his taro patch surrounded by a stone wall. There are several which I will always remember, but one, especially, made me chuckle. It was from an old Hawaiian woman who wrote a letter of complaint to the Land Commissioners: she wrote that in widening what eventually became King Street, near the Kawaiaha`o Church, the road workers had removed the stone wall which surrounded her grass house. And that the cattle which roamed freely had eaten all the grass of her house "as high as their mouths could reach!"

In all those claims there was one poet who wrote lyrically about his little *kuleana* in Hanapepe Valley, here on Kaua`i. He described the boundaries and mentioned the banana trees with fruit on them inviting him to partake, and the birds singing in the morning in the taro patch. I was very moved by this and will always remember his poetry.

The reason I had been asked to do this work was because Miss Conrad hoped to find genealogical information which would help the many Hawaiian people who came to the Archives trying to find out enough about their genealogy to enable them to become claimants for Hawaiian Homes land, or perhaps simply to find their roots. Unfortunately, the claimants recorded in the Native Register were more interested in listing the *konohiki*, or stewards who had been their overseers on the lands on which they worked and lived. Almost no genealogical information was found, but nevertheless, the work has been valuable and helpful to researchers.

I used to work right through the morning up until lunch time because I was so absorbed in my work. I began to notice that one of the young employees used to come into my office and hang about, and I thought it was because she was interested in the work I was doing. But no, she finally "fessed up" that the Hawai`i Government Employees Union had delegated her to come and tell me that under union rules I had to take a coffee break every morning and every afternoon.

I shooed her away and went on working but I began to brood about that union because without my say-so, membership dues in their union were automatically deducted from my paycheck. I never joined their union but, nevertheless, they took my money.

I have forgotten exactly when it was that I had to have a hysterectomy. It may have been in the third year of my employment at the Archives. Although I had passed the menopause, one day at work I had an excessive flow of blood. I decided it would be best to go home, so I drove myself home over the Pali to our little house at Lanikai, where we were living at the time. If I remember correctly, my husband was only working part-time at the Campbell Estate. When I walked into our living room, there was my husband sitting on the sofa very close to one of our female friends in what was obviously a very intimate little visit. There was no confrontation. She excused herself and left, and I don't remember now what passed between my husband and myself.

My husband proclaimed the innocence of his relations with the lady, but I had my own opinion about that.

The result of the flow of blood was that I had to have a hysterectomy to remove a mass of fibroids and so was confined to bed after that for three whole months. During that time I did a lot of reading and thinking, and decided that it was not in my best interests to divorce my husband. I decided that, *inshallah,* I would go on with our marriage and simply accept that men were going to be men and would never be any different. And I recalled that I had an experience early in our marriage which almost cost me my husband, but he forgave me, so who was I to do less than he had. He had always been very good to me and we were friends as well as lovers. (And by the way–to my granddaughters–don't be nosy about that.) What's past is past.

I am a bit vague about whether or not I had finished up the Native Register before this marital contretemps, but I remember that when I finally did finish it, I had an empty feeling as though I'd had a baby. There was more work to be done on translating the Native Testimony which was given on these claims. It was only partially finished and so I completed that work also.

The Native Testimony was as fascinating as the Native Register and I enjoyed doing that as much as I had enjoyed the claims, perhaps even more, because there was much more detail in the Testimony.

As I mentioned earlier, the main reason for doing this huge translation was to help Hawaiian people trace their genealogical background. Of course, we would all like to be able to claim descent from an *ali`i* (in fact, I have never heard anyone claim descent from a *maka`āinana,* the commoners who were the backbone of the Hawaiian nation). But the sad fact is that it is very difficult to trace descent. Due to the calamitous decline of the population after Captain Cook's arrival, when thousands of people died of introduced diseases for which they had no immunity, it is nearly impossible to trace a direct line of descent. Also, in Hawai`i there is the custom of *hānai,* informal adoption, in which family information is not always transmitted. And the custom of *noho,* in which a man and a woman would dwell together for a while and perhaps have a child or two, which they might raise, or which they might pass to a relative to rear.

The only genealogical information which was most carefully preserved was that of the ruling line, the *ali`i.* Even after the missionaries introduced Christian marriage it was already too late for the population to find any record of past ancestors. In a few cases, church records were of help, but often those records were not carefully preserved. However, there are hundreds of names preserved in the Native Register, and, linked with their claims for land in a particular area, this may be of help to genealogical researchers.

I am proud to say that all that work that I did between 1973 and 1976 is now on microfilm at the Archives[1] and I understand that it is much used.

One of the experiences that I had there was a saddening one. One day a woman came in to see me. She was clutching a piece of paper. She seemed to be mentally disturbed but was able to explain to me what she wanted. She asked me to translate the document she handed me, and I did. It was a letter in which Ka'ahumanu, the Hawaiian queen who acted as regent after the death of Kamehameha I in 1819, gave to this woman's ancestors a little sand island near Honolulu Harbor. Apparently this woman's family had been servitors to Ka'ahumanu. The family had held ownership of this little island until the late 1940s.

The powers that be had decided that Honolulu Harbor needed a rear entrance, and also there was the idea of building the "reef runway" at the Honolulu Airport. And so the little island which happened to be in the way was dredged out of existence (probably by my husband, who remembers removing a little house from one of the islands).

So that was the end of Kahaka'aulana (the perch in the current). This poor woman had tried and tried to get some remedy for the loss their family had suffered. They were people who made their livelihood from fishing. But she was ignored at every turn to the point where it had begun to affect her mind. Thinking back on this sad experience I still feel indignation, and wish I could have done something to undo that loss.

The STORY behind the BOOK, *KALUAIKOOLAU*

Quite soon after I began work as Hawaiian Translator at the Hawai''i State Archives I was approached by a writer named Aubrey Janion, who asked me if I would translate a little book entitled, *Kaluaikoolau, the Daring One of the Koolau Cliffs, as told by his wife, Piilani.* This little book, written entirely in the Hawaiian language by John Kahikina Sheldon was published in 1906. It was the story of a historical event which began in July of 1893, in which a leper[1] named Kaluaiko'olau, having taken refuge with his wife and young son in Kalalau Valley on Kaua'i, shot and killed Deputy Sheriff Louis Stolz when Stolz came to the valley to capture him.

The story was written by Pi'ilani, the wife of Kaluaiko'olau (Ko'olau, for short), and describes the period of more than three years when they lived in hiding in Kalalau Valley–this, after her husband shot and killed Stolz and two soldiers of the Provisional Government's army which had gone to the valley to capture Ko'olau, after Stolz was killed. The Provisional Government had just been formed after the overthrow of the Kingdom of Hawai'i in 1893.

The story was well–in fact, sensationally–covered in both the English and Hawaiian language newspapers of the time, and several accounts have been written about it, one of which was by Jack London. Aubrey Janion who, by the way, was a descendant of an earlier Janion who had been in Hawai'i in the early 1800s, was writing a book of historical sketches and wanted to include this story in one of the chapters.

It was agreed that I would do the translation on my own time, and I was given a copy of the Hawaiian original which I took home to study. At first I was not at all sure that I was capable of translating it because the language was rather archaic with long poetic passages using words and allusions unfamiliar to me. I kept asking myself whether I was really understanding the language, but I persevered. Then one night, rather late, when I was curled up in my chair with the book, I found myself beginning to weep over a passage I had just read. Then I knew that I truly was understanding the story. It was the part in which Pi'ilani describes the death of their child, who also had become a victim of the dreaded disease.

When Janion finally received the entire translation, he was so impressed by it that he devoted an entire chapter to it in his book, entitled, *The Olowalu Massacre*. Of necessity, it had to be in abridged form, and most of the poetic language was not shown.

Janion and I were not aware that a translation of the story was, in fact, in existence. I discovered this when a friend of mine who was the historian at the Kaua'i Museum came to the Archives for some research. When I told her what I had been doing with the story of Kaluaiko'olau, she thought she remembered something, and sure enough, when she returned to Kaua'i she found a paper in the collection of the Kaua'i Historical Society written by C. B. Hofgaard, who had lived in Waimea and had operated a store there. He knew Pi'ilani and admired her. His paper told the whole story and confirmed everything that I had translated on my own without knowing about Hofgaard's paper. However, Hofgaard displayed no appreciation for the poetry of the language and, indeed, remarked that it took the Hawaiians three or four words to express something, instead of just *one* word.

I, on the other hand, felt that the poetry and pathos of this story had not been adequately expressed in the abridged chapter in Janion's book, and so I submitted my translation to the Hawaiian Historical Society in Honolulu. They published it in their 1987 Journal of the Hawaiian Historical Society and honored it by giving it the lead position in the Journal, with a photograph of Kalalau Valley on the cover.

This exposure led to some interesting experiences. I received a number of phone calls from people who had read the story and were moved by it. I was approached by Kamehameha Schools and invited to give a number of talks to their adult education groups on the other islands. So I gave several talks which were entitled, "Profile of Courage"[2] on Kaua'i and the other islands. Also, my translation published in the Journal eventually became a book, *The True Story of Kaluaikoolau as Told by His Wife, Piilani*, published in English and in the Hawaiian language in 2001 by the Kaua'i Historical

Society in Līhu`e and distributed by the University of Hawai`i Press in Honolulu.

Another recent development is that a nationally known poet named William Merwin got in touch with me after he read the story in the Journal. We became friends and had a number of discussions about the story, and Pi`ilani, and where she might possibly be buried, as we both felt we would like to go and put a lei on her grave. Unfortunately this never came to pass as no one seems to know where she was buried when she died in 1916.

In 1999 Merwin's long poetic saga entitled *The Folding Cliffs* was published. In his note at the beginning, the poet acknowledges his indebtedness to me. It seems to me that he has created a matrix in which Pi`ilani's story is embedded, giving identity to people and places surrounding this haunting, unforgettable story.

HURRICANE `INIKI

For those of us born in Hawai`i, storms are not major events. We are truly blessed with a climate which is so benevolent I think–hope–that it affects our view of life. Perhaps that climate will enable the eventual change that will come to free some who are now enmeshed in a seemingly impenetrable system of rules that disregard the simple verities of life on an island in the midst of an ocean.

Sometimes those verities become apparent, as on September 11, 1992. Every person who was on Kaua`i on the day `Iniki struck remembers it in their own way. My experiences were not as bad as those of many others, but they are my own and therefore different. Humans have lived under all sorts of circumstances far worse than we experienced, but, in the aftermath of `Iniki, (which means "to pinch or nip repeatedly; tingling, as with cold") our life in our carport was most interesting. Compared to what goes on in the world all the time, it was a picnic. I actually remember it fondly.

I remember other storms, from childhood, but never experienced one in which I felt stark fear. I had missed the full impact of a previous hurricane–Hurricane `Iwa–which occurred ten years before. During that one I happened to be visiting in Honolulu and witnessed the storm from my daughter's apartment. In that period of time high-rise buildings had not yet completely obliterated our view of the harbor and the coastline, and so we witnessed the tumult of the sea's assault from a safe distance.

That earlier storm came without previous warnings. In 1992, although we had warning, I wonder whether very many of us had any real concept of what was about to happen. In my case, having been so lucky that our little farmhouse in Kapahi had escaped damage from the previous storm, I, unknowing, supposed that nothing would happen to us this time either. In 1982, that storm had raged over all of Kaua`i, dismantling the electrical transmission lines and destroying homes, yet the winds had apparently bounced right over our roof. Their full force struck the mountainside behind our house. Sustained blasts had ripped every leaf off the growth on the mountainside behind our house and it was weeks before the vegetation recovered.

Yet the beloved tangerine tree in our front yard, golden with ripening fruit, stood with its fragrant burden unharmed. And our little house suffered no damage whatsoever.

In 1992 we were living in `Ōma`o on the upland slope a few miles above Koloa Town. Our house was sited on the edge of a ravine, overlooking a plantation reservoir, with a beautiful view of the spectacular Hā`upu Range. When we bought that house we never considered how exposed it was to the winds, indeed we welcomed the cooling breezes.

The morning of the storm we arose early and surveyed the probabilities, and decided that we could do nothing to secure ourselves since we did not have enough plywood to protect the full glass exposures which looked to the east. The winds were already blowing hard, and as time went on, the pressure intensified. I had first of all shut our two dogs into one of the bathrooms, and for a while I sat in one of the bedrooms trying to understand what I was seeing. When I looked out of the windows the air could be seen passing by since it was full of particles carried from afar. It is still not possible to remember what it all sounded like, though I have tried.

I walked to the living room, which was oriented to the east, and hearing a new sound, looked up to the eaves over the balcony. To my alarm I saw that the eaves were swaying up and down, so I said to my husband, "It's time we left the house." He at first refused to believe me, but finally we leashed the two dogs, and waiting for a moment of lull, dashed over to our carport.

Most fortunately for us, we had a separate two-car garage. When we bought the unfinished house which we completed, there was no garage attached. When we could afford it, my husband "the engineer" designed a structure which could accommodate two cars and also had a tool-storage workshop room on the windward side. He had designed it with sturdy six-by-six diagonal bracing, and it was roofed with tile to match our house.

We got into our station wagon, putting the dogs into the back, and settled down to wait out the storm. Time passed with agonizing slowness, but one of the marks of that period was the sound of the roof coming off. The whole front part of the roof blew completely over and landed on the other side of the house. A portion of the roof struck our carport but the damage was comparatively minor.

My husband and I held hands, and finally I confessed to him that I was afraid. I have no idea what our beautiful, intelligent German shepherd and our little terrier thought of it all but they were very, very quiet in the back of our station wagon. During the lull of the center of the storm I hastily took them outside to relieve themselves (and also myself). My husband and I wondered what it would be like when the storm came back from the other side, but fortunately the force had lessened and our little shelter held firm with no further damage. We slept in our car that night.

At dawn the next morning I was awakened by the sound of birds chirping in the hibiscus hedge which had sheltered one side of our carport and which had lost all its leaves. I was overjoyed because one of the things that had burdened my mind during the storm was how in the world the birds could survive being blown right out to sea. A long time after, a friend described to me what had happened in her garden. Her house had been built at the bottom of a gulch, and the wind had roared right on overhead and had not damaged her house at all. She said that many birds of all kinds had come into her garden and were sheltering under the bushes.

That same morning our good neighbor Chris came uninvited with his chain saw and cut the branches which had fallen from the trees along our driveway so that we could get out. They offered us shelter in their home, which had suffered almost no damage at all. It was amazing that this had happened, but I finally rationalized that our house must have been struck by a small whirlwind—many of which, I was told later, occurred in the midst of the general storm. Also, the house was on the edge of a bluff so that the wind first struck the bluff, then bounced up and hit us with extra force.

We took shelter for a few nights with the warm-hearted Town family, but eventually we decided to set up housekeeping in our carport. Originally it was enclosed on two sides only, with the workshop on one side, and the carport being open without any door at all. To provide ourselves with some privacy we hung a tarpaulin over the entrance and began to make ourselves cozy. Since we had two beloved pets we were not about to abandon them, and it never occurred to us to move into a hotel as some people did.

We were able to salvage our beds and some pots and dishes from the wreck of the kitchen, and we had the refrigerator moved over to the garage. That was an interesting phenomenon: the wind had opened the refrigerator door, scooped all the contents out (of which we never found any evidence anywhere), then closed the door. A friend loaned us a little gas grill over which we cooked our simple meals. Pots and dishes were washed in a washtub out in the garden. At first, water was not available and it had to be gotten from the water trucks which were stationed around the neighborhoods. Blessedly, the guest bathroom in the ruins of the house was undamaged, and so we were able to use it.

In trying to reconstruct my memories I can not seem to remember when electric power was restored to our neighborhood. It was a memorable day when the water finally flowed out of the taps again.

The most wonderful thing about the experience was people. Like our good neighbor, the doctor, who saw the roof come off our house, and in that dreadful, roaring wind came down to see if he could help us, not knowing we had already taken refuge in our carport. Caring, thoughtful friends and neighbors who came by and said, *Do you have enough water? Here's some fish (or poi, or some vegetables, or a few cans of beer).* For fourteen months we lived in that carport, until our new house was built on the same site, but with different provisions for safety from wind. I remember it as an interesting time, and not at all as a hardship.

ANOTHER BOOK: *KAMEHAMEHA'S WARRIOR, KEKŪHAUPI`O*

Perhaps as a result of the publication of Pi`ilani's story, I was approached some time after its publication by Cappy Summers, a member of the Pacific Translating Committee of the Hawaiian Historical Society. She asked me if I would be interested in undertaking the translation of a very long historical account by Stephen L. Desha. It had been published serially in a Hawaiian language newspaper published by Desha in Hilo, beginning in the early 1920s, and ran with a few interruptions for more than three years. Desha's aim in writing the series was to awaken in his Hawaiian readers an appreciation of their past history and to renew their pride in their race. At this time, when Hawai`i was no longer the Kingdom of Hawai`i but had become the Territory of Hawai`i, there was a real danger of the loss of the Hawaiian language and culture. As mentioned earlier, my own mother had told me that she had been punished as a schoolgirl for speaking a single Hawaiian word. This was also the experience of several other women of her generation whom I knew. They were told, *You are now Americans and should speak English, not Hawaiian.*

I told Cappy that I would be interested in doing the translation, and so the committee arranged for a typed copy of the newspaper articles to be sent me from the Bishop Museum where the account had been preserved, but not translated. So I began a most fascinating and enjoyable period of work in my own home, without compensation, except for the enjoyment I got from following the traces of the story.

A translator must be true to the thought of the writer, and I had already gained experience in translating legal documents which do not allow any deviation from their true content. I fell into the rhythm of Desha's way of thought, and tried to express his writing so as not to interject my own thoughts. I found myself impatient with him sometimes for his adulatory attitude towards the *ali`i,* since it is quite impossible to admire the actions of some of them.

When I had done a chapter (actually these were separate issues of the ongoing history published weekly in *Ka Hoku o Hawai`i,* (The

Star of Hawai'i), I would send it first to Cappy Summers in Honolulu for material content. Then she would send it on to the Island of Hawai'i, where Dorothy Barrere would read it for genealogical and historical content, and then send it back to me with comments, if any. This was a happy and harmonious association which went on for the entire eleven years' duration of the translation.

When the translation was finally done, and I had notified the Hawaiian Historical Society that it was finished, they realized they did not have the funds to publish such a voluminous book. At about that point the Hawai'i State Historic Preservation Division became involved and offered to print fifty copies to be used for research and to be placed in libraries. Then, finally, the Kamehameha School Press was approached and they consented to publish the book, with the valuable assistance of people like Holly McEldowney, who worked with the book designer right to the end–but not until I was able to gain a concession from them that after the expenses of publication were covered, I would receive a twenty per cent royalty.

In September, 2001, I received a phone call from Henry Bennett of the Kamehameha Schools Press. He was quite apologetic about not getting in touch with me before this and that I had not been furnished with the information about the book which was stipulated in my contract. He went on to say that the first edition had been sold out and he had ordered up a second edition. He also went on to say that the book had been put up for an award made annually, called *Ka Palapala Po'okela,* which means The Best Book, and that a party was being planned at the main library in Honolulu on October 19, to which I would be invited.

I was very *kanalua,* or hesitant about going, especially after the September 11 horror, and because flying is not very convenient any more. And also the city life is not for me any more after my long and happy sojourn on Kaua'i. So I waited a while, until I learned that the book would indeed receive some sort of award, and then decided to accept the invitation from the Hawai'i Book Publishers Association. So on the nineteenth I set out from Līhu'e and arrived in Honolulu to be picked up by my young *hānai,* Anita Manning. I had also invited our long time friend Sanford Zalburg,[1] who lives in Honolulu, to attend the party as one of my guests because his step-daughter Noni, living in California, was a great-granddaughter of Stephen L. Desha, and I wanted him to tell her about the award party.

The party was held in the early evening in the courtyard of the dear old library which had been my hangout as a schoolchild, now very beautifully remodeled. The courtyard was full of chairs and there was a table covered with beautiful orchid leis for those who were receiving awards. There must have been at least a hundred guests present because there were several categories of awards. To my surprise and delight I was called up four times to receive an award for my translation of *Kamehameha and His Warrior Kekūhaupi`o*.[2] They were: Winner–Excellence in General Hawaiian Culture; Winner–Excellence in Writing Literature; and also Honorable Mention for Excellence in Non-Fiction Books. I was also called to join a group consisting of the editor, Henry Bennett, and two granddaughters and one grandson of Stephen Desha who were to receive the honor in his memory, plus myself as translator.

Early the next morning I returned to Kaua`i because I had agreed to do another book-signing at Borders that afternoon. I had already done one signing at Borders, but the nicest one was held in the Living Room at the old Wilcox Home in Puhi at Gaylord's Restaurant. I was touched that so many of my long-time friends, plus newcomers, came to that party to have my signature on, in some cases, several copies of *The True Story of Kaluaikoolau, as told by his wife Piilani*. This book has been re-published by the Kaua`i Historical Society, and finally my dearest wish was fulfilled because, this time, the Hawaiian text is included in the back of the book.

My friend Pat Cockett, a talented guitarist, and his vocalist, Manulele, came and presented the song I had composed in 1993 in honor of Pi`ilani for the annual Mokihana Festival Composers Contest in the Hawaiian Music category. This song had won the contest in 1993, the centennial of the events which took place in Kalalau Valley when Ko`olau shot Sheriff Stolz. It has never been professionally recorded, but Pat and Manulele, in just forty-five minutes the day before the book-signing, put together a version of the song, combining Manulele's singing and chanting, and Pat's slack-key guitar. The words are mine, and the very beautiful and haunting melody of the song was composed to go with them by my musical partner Marjorie Taylor, but the presentation by Pat and Manulele was quite as beautiful in a different way.

In connection with the Kamehameha book, when I had completed the translation of the text, I went ahead and put the entire text into my computer, proofread it very carefully with my husband, and saved it on diskettes. I had at one time thought that I wanted the Hawaiian text to be included in the publication, as the old Bishop Museum publications of the Fornander books had been. But the translated text was much too voluminous for that purpose. Some time during publication of my book the diskettes found their way to the Hawaiian Language Department at the University of Hawaiʻi campus at Hilo, where Lokahi Antonio laboriously put in all the diacritical marks. The book has now been published entirely in Hawaiian, in two volumes. No permission had ever been asked of me, but I do not begrudge this publication to them, because I so carefully saved it on diskettes for the very reason of preserving it for the burgeoning population of Hawaiian language students.

I should mention here that the old writings that I worked with for so many years do not have those diacritical markings that came into use after the publication of the wonderful *Hawaiian Dictionary* created by Mary Kawena Pukui and Dr. Samuel Elbert. Desha's writings are entitled *He Moʻolelo Kaʻao no Kekuhaūpiʻo, Ke Koa Kaulana o ke Au o Kamehameha ka Nui.* I am given a "teensy" little credit for preserving his style.

OFFSHOOTS

Interesting projects came my way as a result of my interest in the Hawaiian language. One of these projects came from an introduction by Bob Watts to Tom Armbruster, a young relative of his. To go back before this introduction, perhaps I should tell how it was that I met Bob. Bob was the widower of a member of the Smith-Waterhouse family of Koloa on this island of Kaua`i. His family had a long and distinguished history in the Koloa District. The progenitor of this family arrived in Hawai`i 1842 as a medical missionary, and he and his wife started a family which grew to include a doctor son and a doctor grandson. These three doctors, and another son who figured prominently in the overthrow of the Hawaiian Kingdom, appear in Tom Armbruster's fascinating collection entitled the "Smith Papers."

One of my sassy letters to the local newspaper was the cause of my meeting Bob Watts. I had been rather sarcastic about the changes taking place in the little town of Koloa. A good deal of property in the very small but historic town was owned by the descendants of the family. A man who had been prominent in the commercial development of the island of Maui had been invited to come to Koloa to revitalize the town. I wrote about my fear that development might "Maui-ize" our quiet little island. As a result of this letter, Bob telephoned me and invited me to a reception being held in connection with the completion of the work.

I did not go to the reception but that phone call led to an interesting friendship. Bob was starting a fund which was to be called the Koloa Scholarship Fund, in memory of his wife, a descendant of Dr. James W. and Melicent Knapp Smith, who arrived in Koloa in 1842, and their descendants, Dr. Jared Knapp Smith and Dr. Alfred Herbert and Mabel Palmer Waterhouse. I was honored by being asked to be on the scholarship committee.

As a result of this friendship I was asked to read the "Smith Papers," which were being researched on Kaua`i and in Honolulu at the Mission Children's Society. As Tom Armbruster produced a chapter he would send it to me to read for accuracy in the Hawaiian words used in the letters and papers. This material provided a good deal of historical information.

I was fascinated and amused as time passed that the letters began, from an all-English format, to include a Hawaiian word here and there. What tickled me most of all was, finally, the letter written by Dr. Waterhouse to one of his daughters, then married and living in Iowa, which described what was happening to someone they both knew who was believed to have become a victim of leprosy, or Hansen's disease. That entire paragraph was written in Hawaiian!

The Papers also rounded out for me a good deal of information about the life of The Reverend George Rowell, the founding pastor of the Foreign Church at Waimea. I had been intrigued by mention of him in various publications I had read. I had formed a very favorable opinion of him when I was the Hawaiian Translator at the Hawai'i State Archives, because of a letter that he had written in the Hawaiian language to the Board of Commissioners to Quiet Land Titles. It revealed a man who was caring and interested in seeing that his flock should receive the land they were entitled to apply for. The Smith papers reveal the schism which occurred in the church over Reverend Rowell's scandalous behavior. Certainly, his behavior did not fit the parameters of that period of time, but I still have a warm feeling for him, and it is evident that he was loved by the Hawaiians.

In the year 2000 I was asked by the University of Hawai'i Press if I would be interested in evaluating a translation which had been made of *Anatomia,* by Esther Mookini, a friend of mine. This was a little book which had been translated into Hawaiian for the students at the Lahainaluna School on Maui. It was an interesting project in that it showed that the supposedly primitive Hawaiian language contained a good deal of knowledge about human anatomy and ailments.

LEARNING to COPE

There is a definition of a word in the dictionary which resonates in my mind: It is "cope: 2. to struggle or contend, now usually on equal terms and with some success." Also, there is a valuable Hawaiian phrase: *E ho'omanawanui*, be patient.

The necessity of being a caregiver has come late to me. I have been married to the same man for sixty-four years and if anyone should know him, I should. As stated, Hal was a civil engineer and has worked in many places around the world. I have written how, when our children were young, I stayed at home with them, but when they grew old enough to lead their own lives, I was able to join Hal when he worked in East Pakistan, which became Bangladesh, where we lived for about three years. I traveled to other places with him during his working life, and he has been a loving, kind, and thoughtful husband.

There are times now when I find myself becoming angry and saying cruel things to him. It is necessary for me to stop what I am involved in and tell myself, *This is still the man I married, and who was faithful to me,* although his behavior now is quite often that of a child, rather than the tall, strong man he used to be.

I am at the age of eighty-eight entering a new learning process. What I need to learn is how to feel pity rather than impatience. My ninety-year-old husband[1] has been diagnosed as suffering from "Parkinsonism" and, indeed, he does have the tremor and the shuffling walk. But also, at a recent meeting I heard a speaker describe depression. And I realized that those are exactly the symptoms which afflict my husband. But he can beat me at cribbage quite often, so just where does that fit into the diagnosis?

During my lifetime I have made many dear friends. But now when I need respite, I seem to prefer to be able to retire somewhere quiet with a book or magazine rather than to seek out my friends. I don't know whether this is healthy or not, but for me, reading is an escape hatch.

Actually, there are far worse situations than mine. Our problem began early one morning while I was out walking the dog. I came home to find my husband on the floor and unable to get up. He had fallen in the bathroom and broken his arm and, at first, I was unable to organize any help. I came close to collapse those first few days of coping alone twenty-four hours a day. Finally, I received help from the County Agency on Elderly Affairs, for which I will always be grateful.

But the fixed hours spent by the people sent by the particular organization do not always fit in with my needs. For instance, a small beloved dog shares our lives in our apartment. I, of course, must do all the dog-walking, three times a day, which gives me valuable exercise, although I limit it these days to brisk walks around the hospital grounds across the way. But this means going off and leaving my husband entirely alone. I worry about the possibility of coming back one day and finding he has fallen again. Yet those walks are essential to keeping my equilibrium. And my translating work is also important to keep me centered.

I still am able to continue my work of translating Hawaiian documents and find them just as interesting as I always did. Now at last I have been approached by a young woman of part-Hawaiian ancestry who has learned to speak fluent Hawaiian and at the time she approached me she was teaching in a public school in the Hawaiian language immersion program for the lower grades. She is interested in learning to do the kind of work that I do, and so she comes to me once a week to familiarize herself with legal terms and the pitfalls of doing translating work which might very well turn up in court.

AFTERTHOUGHTS: In the NAME of ALLAH

For the first two years of my life in East Pakistan, now named Bangladesh, I was awakened in the morning by the sound of our *mali* (gardener) invoking the name of Allah in the first of his five obligatory daily prayers. He lived in the servants' quarters at the back of our garden and he was a gentle, hard-working and devout man. He was a world away from the fanatics who created the tragedy in New York on September 11, 2001. And so are millions who share his faith.

When flying on a Pakistan Airlines plane, the pilot will announce, "In ten minutes, *insh'allah,* we will be landing." I think that many Americans who have never had the experience of living in a foreign country do not know how the religious concepts of Muslims are entwined in their minds and everyday life. So many things in our daily life are anathema and prohibited to Muslims. Yet with all these prohibitions the majority of the people of this world-wide religion are able to accommodate themselves to life as lived by non-Muslims. But not so the fanatics.

It disturbs me very much to read the word "War" in relation to the desire to seek out and punish the fanatics. To me, the word "War" calls up thoughts of a contest between two or more nations, in other words, organized entities. How do we define this amorphous miasma of evil which seems to be growing exponentially? If we want to try to remember back just to the beginning of the last century, we can recall a number of happenings which crawled out from under that miasma. The destruction of all those people in the World Trade Towers, although first in magnitude, was not the first such event.

I wonder if we should instead of thinking "War," be thinking of focusing on what the followers of Baha'ullah envision as the Most Great Peace. But then, what of punishment for those who do those dreadful things against all humanity?

As a dream for the future should we not all begin to search our consciences? Ask ourselves, "Did we do anything to provoke this hatred?" If our consciences are clear, then we will have justice on our side and can seek out and punish those who wish to harm us. Yet having done that, we must never let down our guard, knowing that being human is no guarantee of being good.

On SOVEREIGNTY

I have been trying to form some idea of what the future of Hawaiians will be, and I see an over-riding consciousness of being "Of One Blood." Perhaps this is only because I feel it in myself. Ever since those sails were first sighted on the horizon, the streams of consciousness of our ancestors began to be permeated with new and totally different experiences. We are all changed, diluted and yet I feel a stronger pull towards my Hawaiian ancestors than my *haole* ones.

I have said jokingly that in all my whole life, I have heard people claim descent from the *ali'i,* but not one single person has ever proudly stated in my hearing: "My ancestors were *maka'ainana!*"

If the time is taken to read through the Hawaiian newspapers of the time–granted that they were the product of the conquerors–I wonder how much information could be found as to the feelings of the people. The names of my great-grandmother, grandmother, mother and an aunt can all be found on the *Aloha 'Āina* declaration.

Yet land as a commodity, which it became at the time of the Mahele, began to pass from Hawaiian hand to Hawaiian hand, and then, from Hawaiian hands to the *haole,* the *Pakē* (Chinese), the *Pukiki* (Portuguese), and other races as they arrived in *Hawai'i nei,* the homeland of Hawai'i. I have in my files hundreds of documents from the Bureau of Conveyances which I have translated over forty years, and what I have seen is the inexorable passage of land out of the hands of the native-born.

This depressing knowledge has kept me from fully engaging in the sovereignty movement because I do not have confidence that when it comes to self-interest, those who seek sovereignty will cling to possession of the land. In my childhood and early years there was stalwart David of Punalu'u, who wore his red *malo* and worked in his taro patches. Who among us now can return to the stark simplicity of life in the taro patch?

"Hele ka la i ka pō, ahiahi no'u."
The day goes on into night–for me it is evening.
–"Uncle" Morris Dudoit

`elima / five

ET CETERA

From the PAPERS of
FRANCES N. FRAZIER

RESUMÈ

MRS. FRANCES N. FRAZIER, HAWAIIAN TRANSLATOR
September 2003

RESUMÈ OF BACKGROUND IN HAWAIIAN LANGUAGE

I was born in Honolulu, Hawai`i, July 6, 1914.

Mother, part-Hawaiian, part-English. Father, New England ancestry (English/Dutch). English was spoken at home. Hawaiian was not spoken at home, although both my parents understood the Hawaiian language. My mother was punished as a school child for speaking Hawaiian (the experience of many children at that period of time.) My father, a ship captain employed by the Inter-Island Steam Navigation Company, had Hawaiian crews, and spoke Hawaiian.

1932: Graduated from McKinley High School and then attended a business college in Honolulu. From there I was sent to work at the Board of Water Supply and remained there for more than eight years.

1937: Married, started family life.

1950s: At Bishop Museum was one of several volunteers who typed for Mrs. Mary Kawena Pukui, at that time Hawaiian Scholar at the Bishop Museum. We were inspired and encouraged by her to learn the Hawaiian language. Before her death she was designated a Living Treasure of the State of Hawai`i.

This experience was the beginning of my interest in and study of the Hawaiian language.

For over one year worked as a typist for Mrs. Kulamanu Williams, now deceased, in preparing a book entitled "Teach Yourself Hawaiian." Mrs. Williams never published her book but I learned enough grammar and had become so interested in the Hawaiian language that Dr. Samuel Elbert, Chairman of the Department of Asian and Pacific Languages at the University of Hawai'i (and co-author with Mary Kawena Pukui of the Hawaiian-English Dictionary published by the University of Hawai'i Press) permitted me to audit his second and third year courses in the Hawaiian language at the University of Hawai'i, finding it was unnecessary for me to take the first-year course.

At about this same time I assisted with the editing and preparation for publication of the English-Hawaiian version of the Pukui-Elbert Dictionary. It appeared in 1964, and the assistance of myself and others is credited in the Acknowledgements.

I was asked by Marian Kelley who was Dr. Kenneth Emory's assistant, in the Department of Anthropology, Bishop Museum, to translate the explanatory texts in Hawaiian which accompanied some of the text of "The Missionary Census of 1835" by Robert C. Schmitt, Pacific Anthropological Records, Number 20.

EMPLOYMENT

After marriage and later resignation from Board of Water Supply I did volunteer work at the Bishop Museum (as above) and for a couple of years was employed as Administrative Assistant to the Astronomer at the Planetarium at Bishop Museum, during which time I was allowed to work on translation of material at the Bishop Museum, at times when work at the Planetarium permitted.

1963 – 1968: Went to live in former East Pakistan with my husband, a Civil Engineer who was employed there. After two and a half years we returned to Hawai'i for a vacation and were prevented from returning until the end of the war which divided West Pakistan from what is now Bangladesh.

1968 – 1973: Translations of deeds, etc., when needed, for Long & Melone Title Insurance Co.

1969 – 1973: As above for Title Guaranty of Hawai'i, Inc.

1973 – 1976: Employed by the State of Hawai`i as Hawaiian Translator at the Hawai`i State Archives, under Miss Agnes Conrad. For three years my major task was to translate the entire Native Register, consisting of nine volumes averaging 500 or more pages each, which I completed. The Native Register consists of claim letters written in the Hawaiian language in the period of 1845 to about 1855, by native Hawaiian claimants of lands, who addressed their claims to the Board of Commissioners to Quiet Land Titles in the Hawaiian Islands. All present day land titles in Hawai`i stem from this period and these claims, as well as the Mahele awards. I also translated portions of the "foreign" Testimony on the afore-mentioned claims.

In addition to this work, I translated upon request anything in the Hawaiian language including legal documents of all kinds: wills, court testimony, etc.

My husband, now retired, is a Civil Engineer with a degree from the University of California at Berkeley. He had also attended the University of Hawai`i, where he took a course in Hawaiian land surveying. When I was beginning my translating work he was helpful with the correct terms used in land survey.

1976 to date:

In 1976 I resigned from the Archives in order to live on Kaua`i where I have continued to translate deeds, leases, patents, awards, land surveys, wills, probate and other court documents for the following clients: Title Guaranty of Hawai`i, Inc.; Carlsmith Ball Wichman Murray Case & Ichiki; Hana Ranch, Inc.; Stanley H. Roehrig; Ashford & Wriston; Sterry Mah and Gallup; Case, Kay & Lynch; James R. Judge; and numerous individuals.

I HAVE APPEARED AS EXPERT WITNESS IN THE FOLLOWING COURTS:

July, 1979, in Honolulu before Judge Robert Won Bae Chang.

February, 1982, in Hilo before Judge Kubota.

October, 1984, in Kealakekua, Kona before Judge De Silva.

In addition, in October, 1984, was excused by Judge Kubota from appearing on another case because of my prior acceptance in his court as expert witness.

In August 2001, in Wailuku before Judge Shackley F. Raffetto, for Carlsmith Ball LLP.

In 2003 I was asked by Dennis King of Deeley, King & Pang to translate some documents in connection with a case between the City and County of Honolulu as Plaintiff vs. Claire Kehaulani Ayau; Maxine C. Horton, etc. He asked me to appear in court if necessary. On July 30, 2003 I was informed that the case had been settled out of court apparently to the satisfaction of all parties.

PUBLICATIONS OF OTHER TRANSLATING WORK

"The True Story of Kaluaiko'olau, or Ko'olau the Leper." This was written in Hawaiian by Pi'ilani, wife of Ko'olau, and was published in Hawaiian by John Kahikina Sheldon in 1906. My translation of this story was first published in the "'Olowalu Massacre," a book of historical vignettes by Aubrey Janion in 1976, and also appeared in The Journal of Hawaiian History published in 1987. It was re-published by the Kaua'i Historical Society in 2001.

"Kamehameha and His Warrior Kekūhaupi'o." A series of articles were written and published in a Hawaiian language newspaper in the early 1920s by Rev. Stephen L. Desha because of his desire to restore the pride of the Hawaiian people in their history and culture. My translation of thee articles has been published by the Kamehameha Schools Press and is now available in bookstores.

AWARDS

In September 2000, I, along with several others, received the Kaonohi Award "In the Spirit of Dr. Alexander Kohiai Kaonohi." The award was presented at a gathering at Washington Place, in Honolulu.

In the year 2001 I received three awards from the Hawai`i Book Publishers Association, presented at a gathering at the Hawai`i State Public Library in Honolulu:

> For my book "Kamehameha and His Warrior Kekūhaupi`o," for
> Excellence in Writing Literature – Winner
> Excellence in General Hawaiian Culture – Winner
> Excellence in Nonfiction Books – Honorable Mention

In the year 2002 I received an award from the Hawai`i Book Publishers Association at a gathering at the Hawai`i State Public Library in Honolulu:

"The True Story of Kaluaikoolau: As Told by his Wife, Piilani" – Honorable Mention

LETTER from ZELIE
DUVAUCHELLE SHERWOOD

May 28, 1969

Dear Frances,

Luckily my sister forwarded your letter to me here on Oahu.

I left Molokai the morning of May 20th and naturally did not receive your letter. I wouldn't have received it until after July 14th, since I am going on a cruise to the South Pacific, leaving on the Mariposa on Saturday, May 31st. Amory will be going with me. Come and see us if you can. People may come aboard at 3:00 P.M.

I don't mind your calling me Zelie and am happy that you have asked me for help. I will be glad to help you any time you need help. You don't need much teaching. Please make a copy of this Hawn. instrument for me. You can mail to me to Molokai and it'll be there when I come back. I usually make notes of unusual words and add them to a vocabulary that I am compiling.

Sorry that I am sending your letter back but I thought it best if I made notes right on the paragraph in question. I would suggest that you ask Mary Melone to get you a copy of an English lease of about the date of the lease you translated. This will give you an idea of the words used at that time.

You must know some Hawaiian other than from the university under Sam Elbert. Mrs. Pukui is an exceptionally good teacher. She has great knowledge of the language. I don't know Elbert so I can not say anything of his teaching of Hawaiian.

You do exceptionally well for someone who has just learned the language. Your translation is very good. It shows a background of Hawaiian and a thorough knowledge of the language. It is gratifying to find someone who is able to translate. I am glad Mary Melone found out about you and sends you translation to do for her. Practice is the best teacher.

You must be the friend Mary Melone talks about who has a place on the beach in Honouliwai. I, too feel like I know you, even though we have never met. Too bad I haven't been home when you were on Molokai. We should be meeting soon.

I believe that I have covered everything since I can't think of anything further to say so I shall close now. I am glad you wrote instead of phoning because we could not have covered everything by phone.

Me ke aloha,
(Signed) Zelie

P.S.: I will use your envelope at another time.

LETTER from KENNETH P. EMORY

BERNICE P. BISHOP MUSEUM

P. O. Box 6037, Honolulu, Hawai`i 96818 . Telephone 847-3511

August 15, 1972

TO WHOM IT MAY CONCERN:

Mrs. Frances N. Frazier is a translator of the Hawaiian language who was formerly employed by the Committee for the Preservation of the Hawaiian Language and Culture. One of her duties at that time was to assist in the work of preparation of the Pukui-Elbert English-Hawaiian Dictionary. Her name appears, with others, in the preface to the dictionary in the credits given by the authors.

She is at present on the staff of the Bishop Museum as administrative assistant at the Science Center.

She has done for the Museum a translation consisting of five volumes of a historical account of King Kamehameha the First, taken from the Hawaiian language newspaper Ka Na'i Aupuni. In connection with this translation she had the opportunity of comparing her work with that done separately, in a partial translation of the same material by E. Sterling, now deceased. This comparison showed a consensus in meaning, although the two translations were done completely independently of each other.

She also assisted in a portion of the translation of an account entitled "Kekuhaupi'o," taken from the Hawaiian language newspaper, Ka Hoku o Hawai`i.

(Signed) Kenneth P. Emory
Senior Anthropologist

LETTER to my NEPHEW

July 10, 1997

Dear Allan,

In your loss of your father you must be searching your memories, and after talking to Cindy[1] this afternoon I decided to send you a copy of the family history that I have been compiling.

Julian[2] and I never talked about our family history and I don't know how much he actually knew, because our mother never shared very much with me and probably not with him, either. So I hope that the background information I can share will be of help to you. It is of course wound about with my own and Harold's family, but there is a lot of family background too.

One of my lifelong memories is of your father as a little boy running in his funny little tippy-toe way back and forth on the long veranda at the Punchbowl house in which we lived, gone for many years now since the apartment building was constructed. He was the *poki'i,* the youngest one, and our older brother Dick was a little too old to be a playmate, since there was a difference of more than eight years (I think – I'll have to look that up.)

When I spoke to your mother this evening we talked about putting his ashes out in the sea at Lanikai, and how very appropriate I thought that would be. We, with our older brother "Dickie" took our mother's ashes out there in our boat. When my father died, Julian and I took his ashes out there, too, out between the two islands called Mokulua. They specified this in their wills.

The sea at Lanikai was always a very special place for your father, and for me too. We sailed and fished and he ran his speedboat there, and it was a wonderful time of growing up in freedom, the memory of which I cherish. I am sure you have your memories of that place too.

I need a little time to finish up some proof-reading I am doing on a book I expect will be published, and as soon as I find the time I will add a few more things to my family account and send a copy to you.

In the meantime, I hope that you and Cindy and Alex[3] will find the time to come and visit us on Kaua'i. Stephanie is occupying the cottage but there's a bed in my office, and a couple of couches that are comfy enough, and we would love to have you come and stay with us.

Me ke aloha pu mehana,
(Signed) Your Aunt Frances

LETTER to the FORUM

September 28, 1999

To the Forum[1] and all those earnest and well-meaning planners:

All the calculations and arguments about growth overlook one thing which seems to me to be the very crux of the matter.

Growth brings the need for more dwelling space and infrastructure to accommodate those who will serve the visitors who are so hopefully projected for the future. And of course there will have to be more hotels and more time shares to accommodate the growing number of visitors.

Fine, splendid, you can do that. But my question is: how do you plan to expand the beaches, the streams, the mountain trails and valleys to accommodate, for instance, the "de facto" population of 111,390 in the year 2020? And if you can't figure that out, can you at least figure out what else you can offer the visitors?

Do you have entree into the grand scheme of creation which made all our beautiful beaches? Can you increase their size commensurate with the need to accommodate all those folks in 2020 and who knows how far beyond?

Can you persuade the Forces that created the Wailua and Hule'ia and other rivers to widen and lengthen those rivers to accommodate more and more kayaks and other craft?

And what about the valleys of Nā Pali? Can you persuade those Forces to make a few more of those to accommodate everyone who wants to go there?

Seems to me that if we can't even persuade the government to fix the *luas* [toilets (pits)] at Ke'e beach we had better lower our sights, and think of some other way to survive on this little island, besides inviting a lot more people here.

If you don't accommodate every single one of them and they have to make reservations a year or two in advance, maybe those who are able to come will appreciate us a lot more because they will know that they are chosen to be in a special place, and that the aloha they receive will be genuine, not manufactured somewhere else.

165

Those of us who were born in Hawai'i may remember Lau Yee Chai, a famous and delightful Chinese restaurant in Waikīkī. The owner of the restaurant had a disagreement with his wife and she took over the restaurant and threw him out. Some months later a tiny hole-in-the-wall chop-suey joint opened on Mauna Kea Street in Chinatown. In the window was a little sign which said:

"Tree no choosy bird; bird choosy tree."

At what point will the birds no longer choose our tree because all the roosting places are full and there's no more room?

(Signed) Frances N. Frazier
Līhu'e, Kaua'i, Hawai'i

JACK LONDON SOCIETY SYMPOSIUM PAPER: 'Profile of Courage'

Paper, "Profile of Courage" presented to members and guests of the Jack London Society Symposium,[1] Kaua`i, Hawai`i, October 2002. (Also presented to Elderhostel travelers to Kaua`i in "Land & Power" program classes 1997-1998, as Instructor for Pacific Islands Institute through Hawai`i Pacific University–Elderhostel)

Based on and quoted from "The True Story of Kaluaiko`olau, As Told by His Wife, Pi`ilani"
Written in Hawaiian by Pi`ilani, the wife of Kaluaiko`olau
Translated by Frances N. Frazier

This true story which belongs to Kaua`i has been told and retold. It contains ugly elements: leprosy which separated families, murder, an armed invasion and bombardment of a peaceful valley, and the death of Ko`olau and his little son. The culminating events in the story begin in 1893, the very year of the overthrow of Queen Lili`uokalani and the theft of the kingdom of Hawai`i by a small group of American businessmen.

Yet the tragedy is subsumed by the lyrical account of enduring love, patient care, and a strength of character which enabled Pi`ilani, the heroine, to survive, to surmount the difficulties and tragedies, and to write their story in hauntingly beautiful language which preserves many poetic words now regrettably archaic.

"On a certain day there came to our house at Mana a man named Pokipala who worked for the government, who had come to fetch Ko`olau to be seen by the doctor because he had been observed by one who had suspected that he had leprosy, the royal disease, the disease that separated families. My people of the same blood you cannot conceive of the profound gloom of my thoughts at this time and those of you who have experienced this will know of the grief, and I joined those of you who have shouldered the burden and I know of the piercing thrusts of grief . . ."

Because the policy of the government had changed and lepers were no longer allowed to be accompanied by helpers to exile on Molokai, Ko`olau and Pi`ilani, who had sworn never to be parted, determined to take refuge in isolated Kalalau Valley.

"At sunset on a certain day when the wings of darkness spread over the ridges and rows of cliffs of our beloved land, in the winter of 1892, we loaded ourselves and our belongings on horseback and in the loneliness and awesomeness of the night turned towards the trail which would descend into Kalalau, leaving behind our 'birth sands', without knowing when we would see them again or breathe the comforting air of our birthplace. . ."

When Deputy Sheriff Stolz[2] pursued Ko`olau to Kalalau with the intention of taking him prisoner or killing him, he was shot and killed by Ko`olau.

"A gun was heard being cocked, and at this moment my husband protected me by putting me behind him, and with a flash of powder his gun was fired, and we heard the voice of the *haole* saying, '*Hu*, it hurts.' The reverberations of the gun sounded everywhere, spreading the news of this terrible thing done on this unforgettable night. At this time we saw Lui's companion who had been with him as my husband had said; this was Paoa, a man who had been arrested by Lui on the mountain. Paoa ran to the place where the *haole* had been struck by the firing of the gun, while Ko`olau was going there, and began to beat the *haole*. Ko`olau was angry with him, saying he should be careful or he would kill him. At this time my husband called me to go away and while I was doing this I glimpsed Lui kneeling, holding the gun, and Paoa shouted, 'He is going to shoot,' and this was the moment my husband fired the second bullet and Lui died... ."

Ko`olau's friends wanted to join him in defending against the attack which they knew would come, but he advised them not to stay, saying,

"Yes, it is indeed possible that my death is coming, what of it? Death is the end of all men, and man only dies once. And who would not be killed, with a warship coming here with soldiers and arms; therefore how shall Ko`olau alone escape?"

Ko`olau advised Pi`ilani to join their friends and go to the shore, but she refused to leave him and so they and their little son went to take refuge on a high promontory of the valley.

"While we were sitting there we heard the shouting of voices, and at this place, my friends, you will learn of one of the wicked and wrongful deeds which the Provisional Government did with great arrogance. They and all the people whom the power of the Provisional Government had sent to capture Ko`olau, by their actions became despised by those born with Christian consciences. On the arrival of these P. G. soldiers with bloodthirsty hearts at Kahalanui where we had been living, when they understood no one was there, because of their rage they began to burn the houses and all the belongings. . .

They stupidly thought by this that they would frighten and capture my husband. . .

Because of these actions my husband and I were filled with rage, and if perhaps we could have gotten some of them we would have wrung their bones and fed them to the fire.

Until this day I m not done brooding over these plundering, burning, thieving P. G. *kolea*, the birds who came to fatten on our land, who came as wanderers and arrogantly lived on the sweet breast of our native land. . ."

In spite of the bombardment of their hiding place, they escaped after a few days and moved to another part of the valley, and the army gave up its efforts and departed. The disease first took the life of their little son, and then after a while, Ko`olau also died and in a secret place she dug his grave with her bare hands and a small tool. As he had asked, she buried his rifle with him.

She remained in hiding a while longer, but homesickness drew her back to Kekaha where she was reunited with Ko`olau's mother, and where the High Sheriff absolved her of blame. After she had climbed up out of that sheltering valley she paused at the top and gazing at its beauty, she sent her love in a poetic chant to all the refuges in the valley which she had shared with her husband and child. She names all those beloved places, and concludes:

"And, O, the succoring, hospitable valley of Kalalau! You are surrounded by my love, you are the recipient of all my desires, until my end. I am going on a road that leaves you behind, leaving in the intense fragrance of your wilderness the bones of our beloved ones. I leave them to sleep gently in your peace. Yours is the hiding, the secret hiding, the secret hiding that is taken, the secret hiding that is taken forever. Overwhelming love to you. You will be hidden from my sight, yet always in my heart I will gaze in remembrance. It has been lit, it can never be extinguished in a great flood. Farewell, my footsteps take their course and I bear upon me constant love. So it shall be!"

`*eono* / six

SPECIAL ADDITION:

THE DIARY and SHIPS' LOG
(Condensed)

of Richard Nelson

b. 1876 – d. 1960

THE DIARY and SHIPS' LOG
of RICHARD NELSON,
Master Mariner and Captain

This document in its complete form is on file (with photos) at the Hawai`i State Archives, archive of Frances N. Frazier, as typed from the original version by Nelson's granddaughter Stephanie Frazier. Spelling, including the lack of Hawaiian diacritical markings, and information is reproduced here "as is" from the archived document. Exceptions are portions marked with ellipses (. . .) where "The Diary and Ships' Log" has been condensed, occasional corrections of punctuation, and the addition of bracketed [ ] information judged helpful to the reader.–Ed.

From all accounts, I was born on 08/22/1876 in a boarding house on the coast of New Jersey at a place called at that time Ocean Beach, but many years later its name was changed to "Belmar." It was on the banks of the Shark River, and my mother was there on summer vacation. I was taken there once a few years later and I saw what the place looked like and again, in 1934, I passed through Belmar on an automobile trip but could not recognize any place that I had seen before.

My father. . .(after joining the Scovill Mfg. Co.) was continuously employed until his retirement 40 years later. He worked his way up so that he was the purchasing agent for the company. . .

I attended the usual schools and at the time I left school, I was attending the Waterbury High School. . . I do not remember what grade I was in, but I do remember that I never liked school at any time. After leaving the high school, my father wanted me to go to a business school. He bought me the books and I attended for one day and then quit as I had no desire to become an office worker. I was sent to a boarding school. . .for one or two terms but did not like it there and did not return to finish the course.

I worked at Scovill Co. on a machine that was an automatic lathe, making small articles out of brass bar stock up to about one inch in diameter. I also operated a turret lathe, also making small articles out of brass, but this machine was not automatic but operated by hand. I also worked at electric house wiring as a helper at first and later doing jobs by myself. . .

I had always wanted to "go to sea." The idea probably came from reading sea stories by J. Fenimore Cooper and W. Clark Russell, all of which I got from the Waterbury public library where I had a card and took out many books on the subject of ships and sailing. After some objections by the family, my father agreed to help me get started, and we decided on trying to get on the New York Nautical School ship "St. Mary's," then operated by the school system of the City of N.Y. As only boys who lived in NY [New York] State could get in there, I had the help of an uncle, George W. Nelson, who lived in NYC [New York City] on W. 48ᵗʰ St. As I never liked the name Smith [Smith was surname at birth], I had my name legally changed to Richard Nelson and became the ward of my uncle. . . (I) was admitted to the school ship through the influence of my uncle and remained there during the years 1894-95, graduating in the later year as the head of the class. . .

'ST. MARY'S' VESSEL TRAINING in 1894-5

The "St. Mary's" was a small three-mast full rigged ship belonging to the Navy and loaned to the city. It had gun ports on one deck but the guns were not used. It was outfitted and officered by the Navy but operated by the city school system. During the winter and spring a temporary wooden sectional house was erected on a deck to use as school rooms. In the summer, the house was removed and put on the deck. The ship was fitted for going to sea and towed to Glen Cove. . . through Hellgate and the Long Island Sound. After the towboat left her at anchor in Glen Cove, the boys were trained in handling sails, boats and seamanship. After a couple of weeks of this training, the ship sailed to New London and later across Atlantic to ports in Europe, the Azores and Madeira Island.

The boys slept in hammocks slung from iron hooks in the gun deck beams. . . The meals were served on portable tables in the gun deck, which were scrubbed with sand and canvas each day and were always clean.

During the winter, the boiler of the steam launch was hoisted out of the launch and lowered down in the hold of the ship and there provided the only heat on the whole ship. It also provided the steam used to heat the cold water in the bathroom on deck where the boys were required to take a hot water bath every Saturday night. . . Three times a day before meals all the boys were required to go up the rigging on one side of the muster, through the "tops" and down on the other side for exercise. This was not done when at sea, only in port at New York.

At various times, I was assistant to the sailmaker and "rated" as "sailmaker mate." I learned to sew canvas, which has been of great benefit to me ever since. I always carry my sewing kit of "palm," "needles" and twine wherever we are living, and have saved myself many dollars by making my own bags, covers, tarpaulins and awnings.

For most of the time, I was also a "ship writer" and had a small room office and kept the records and made out the liberty lists of those entitled to go ashore at various ports where liberty was allowed. The food was only fair but plentiful. At one time, the steward who contracted for food got such a bad lot that the boys refused to handle the ship until better food was provided. It was a small-sized mutiny, but it worked and better food was obtained.

One time on beating up(river) to New London, Conn. [Connecticut] The ship went aground on a mud bank near one of the big hotels along the shore. No damage was done, but it provided a chance to train the boys in carrying out anchors and rigging gear to haul the ship off the mudbank with assistance of two boats. At one time during the operation, the boys were made to rush from one side of the deck to the other to roll the ship in the mud, and it worked, for at high tide, we got the ship afloat again and sailed on up to New London. That was the only time the ship got ashore, but at Porta Delgada, Azores, we were caught by a gale wind from the south and lay for two days with both anchors down and all the chain we had out. The ship's stern was only a short distance from a stone breakwater, and if the anchors and chain had failed us, the ship would have been over the rocks in a few minutes. . . We got out of that safely, but it was all hands from the captain down worried as long as it lasted.

The ports we called at were Layal and Porta Delgada in the Azores; and Lisbon and Gibraltar on the mainland and to Funchal, Madeira on the way home. We made two summer voyages but did not get to England as had been the custom on former voyages. The years were 1894-95. During those years, we had some officers supplied by the Navy who later became admirals. Capt. McGowan was the commander on the first voyage and Will Field was in command the second year. The second lieutenant was Andrew Long and the third lieutenant was Henry A. Wiley, who taught navigation. I was a good learner and tried to improve whatever knowledge of navigation I have. I afterward met him when he was an admiral and in command of a ship at Honolulu.

THE 'TILLIE E. STARBUCK'

After leaving the "St. Mary's," I returned home to Waterbury with my canvas clothes bag and hammock and with the assistance of my father, began looking for a ship to get further training on. Due to the kindness of a boyhood friend of my father. . . , I was able to get shipped on as "boy" or "ordinary seaman" on the full rigged three skysail yard ship, "Tillie E. Starbuck," then taking on cargo at a pier on South St. The ship was owned by Dearborn and Co., who later formed the American Hawaiian Steamship Line. The sailing ships owned by this firm were the beginning of the ships used in the "sugar trade" between Hawai`i and N.Y. and the East Coast. The steamers of the American Hawaiian Line ran for many years between these ports carrying sugar and general cargo from N.Y. After the Hawaiian sugar planters started their own sugar refinery in Crockett, near San Francisco, and the Matson line started hauling their sugar, the Am. Hwn. Co [American Hawaiian Company] did not send its ship to Hawai`i any more.

The "Starbuck" was the first all iron (not steel) sailing ship within the U.S. She was built at Chester, PA and was a very well built and strong ship. . . The crew lived in the forward house which was also built of iron. Next to the carpenter shop was the carpenter's room, with two bunks in it and a room for the "boatswains" with two bunks in there. On the first voyage, I lived in the carpenter's room and on the second voyage, I was promoted to be a "boatswain" and lived in the other room.

The captain was Eben Curtis of Searsport, Maine, a very fine man who knew his business and how to handle his ship and men. He always treated me in the best manner possible. He took an interest in training me to be a ship's officer and gave me a chance to work at navigation during the two voyages. When I joined the ship, I asked the captain to get me a good sextant, which he did at a pawn shop on South St. For $120, a very good bargain, as I have that sextant yet and have used it on several voyages later, when I was in command of small steamers and tow boats. . . On the first voyage, my father sent two barrels of apples, one green and one red, on board and as I had no place to store them, I turned them over to the steward for use in the cabins. I also got a few now and then. . .

The mate (on the first voyage that I was on) was a Mr. Donald F. Nicholson. He was a big man and weighed over 250 lb. He was a good seaman and knew his business. He had been an amateur fighter in his earlier years and claimed to have fought with the famous John L. Sullivan, the champion for many years. . . He could handle any two sailors, and there was never any trouble with the crew as long as I was on the ship. Mr. Nicholson. . .when we returned to New York, . . . left the ship. . .

. . . To get back to the "Tillie Starbuck," I brought my "sea chest" which I had made in the attic of our home in Waterbury on board after the ship was loaded and laying to at the dock on South St. [New York City] . . .The sails had been "bent" by the longshoremen and the hatches "battened down," so the ship was ready for going to sea except for the crew. The day of sailing, the crew was put on board, mostly drunk, with a few men sober enough to help get away from the dock.

A tow boat came alongside and took us out from the dock and down the East River. When we had left the dock, the mate started setting sail on the ship and by the time we were through the "narrows," the ship was going so fast with a fair wind that the tow boat could not keep the tow line tight, so the captain told them to let go the line and we sailed out of the channel with the pilot in charge until we were off the pilot station near the lightship. After the pilot left us, we started to secure the anchors on deck and get the ship ready for a long voyage. We had good weather so far as I can remember and made the usual course used by ships bound around Cape Horn. We passed through the N.E. and S.E. tradewinds and sailed down by the east coast of South America well off shore. Somewhere in south latitude, we met a vessel bound back to New York and as it was fine weather, the captains had a boat lowered and sent mail back by the ship. I sent letters that were safely delivered when this vessel reached port...

RETURN to HONOLULU

Arriving in Honolulu after a smooth passage, we were towed in to Brewer's Wharf and the crew started discharging the captain's cordwood [purchased on "his own account" for ballast] after we had a few steamer-loads of sugar on board to act as ballast. The ship was moved to various wharves around the harbor, gathering the various lots of sugar and when nearly loaded was "moored" out in the harbor, where the final lots of sugar were loaded on board from steamers alongside. While in Honolulu, I spent the Sunday exploring around the town and with the carpenter walked up Nuuanu St. to the "pali," then the end of the road, there being only a horseback trail down the other side. The distance was about seven miles up and the same back. We walked all the way and down the trail to the bottom on the other side of the Pali.

After we were loaded with sugar and the sails "bent," we hauled over to the Pacific Mail wharf and took on fresh water and stores and pigs and chickens for the captain's table. His family was left behind in Honolulu and they returned to Portland by steamer. The pilot, Capt. McCanley (whose place I took when he retired in 1919) took the ship out to sea by sailing right from the wharf, first setting the sails while still fast to the dock. Then, letting go the boss line and holding onto the stern line, he sailed out without a towboat. A very neat job, only possible where wind and channel conditions made it possible.

BACK to NEW YORK by GOING AROUND CAPE HORN

The voyage home to New York was a fine weather voyage, even around Cape Horn, where we had a light westerly wind and a smooth sea, a most unusual condition. The captain sailed within sight of the land and he pointed out to me a rock that he said was the real Cape

Horn. I took a picture, which is probably one very few taken of that cape from the south. It was so far away that it does not show up very good in the print.

. . . We had a nice run up to the equator in the south Atlantic Ocean and when somewhere off the West Indies one day during a calm, with all sails set, a small cloud appeared on the horizon, and at this time of the year, it indicated a tropical squall. . . . . .the captain said to wait till we could see what was in the squall. He soon found out, as the wind hit the ship on the forward side of the sails and for a few minutes, we went astern faster than she ever went ahead. Within a few minutes, before anything could be done, all the sails were split or blown away and all the masts above the topmost heads were broken off, and they and the sails and rigging and yards were hanging down over the deck and over the side. The squall only lasted a few minutes, but in that time the ship was left in a mess, with no means of going anywhere.

No one was hurt and at once we started to get the wreck cleared away, get up new sails and secure the broken pieces of masts and yards. We had enough spare yards and sails to partly re-rig the ship, and after a week's work of repairs, with all hands working all day and no watches at night, we sailed into New York without any further trouble. . . (and) were towed to the sugar refinery dock to unload the cargo of sugar.

I went home to Waterbury for as long as the ship was unloading and being reframed, about three months. After being refitted, they loaded general cargo for Sydney, Australia. I came to New York and joined the ship again. The mate, Mr. Nicholson, had left and returned to Honolulu overland. We had a new Mate, a Mr. Leonard. . .(who) was sullen and sulky most of the time. The time of the refitting of the ship was in December 1896 and cold. The "lanyards" of the rigging had all been replaced by new hemp rope and had been set up as tight as possible in the cold weather.

AROUND CAPE HORN AGAIN in JANUARY 1897

We left New York about January 2 or 3 and after a day or two we ran into the Gulf Stream and much warmer weather. Also, we ran into a Northeast storm of hurricane proportions. The wind blowing against the Gulf Stream caused a very high and rough sea. The wind must have been at lest 100 miles per hour. Soon the sails. . .began to blow away out of the gaskets (lashings). The new lanyards of the rigging became slack because of the warm weather (or change in temperature) and were of no support to the masts. The lower masts, being of iron, stood up all right, but most everything above the lower mast heads, along with the yards and what was left of the sails came down and were hanging either on deck or over the side. The fore topsail yard was hanging outside the starboard rail, and with the continued rolling and banging about, it broke the starboard bulwark or rail, and soon the whole starboard rail from the forecastle to the afterhouse was torn off and lost overboard.

As the storm was so bad that nothing could be done at the time, the captain called all hands aft to the cabin and everyone expected the ship to go down. . . However, the ship was made of tough iron plates and they stood the beating all right. . .

During the first night of the storm, the carpenter and myself were the only ones remaining in the forward house. . . the carpenter went down into the main hold through a ventilator with a lantern to see if the ship was taking any water. I remained on the rail around the main mast, where the ventilator was, and kept the canvas cover on it while he was down below. He found that there was no water in the bilges, which showed that the ship was not leaking. . . it was a great relief to us to know (this). . . The next day the wind moderated a little, although there was a very rough sea running.

The mate got the crew out and we started to clean away the wreck. . . We were able to get up and "bind" some spare sails to the fore and main yards. The captain sailed the ship to near Bermuda Island, where we were seen and towed into the harbor of Hamilton near the navy yard. We remained there for several weeks at anchor until a towboat. . .was sent down from New York and were towed back to N.Y. without any further trouble.

At that time, I went home to Waterbury again and waited until the ship was repaired and refitted with new rigging and sails. I was called by the captain to be a witness at the insurance inquiry and when the repairs were finished, I came back to N.Y. and rejoined the ship. . . and started our voyage toward Sydney, NSW [New South Wales, Australia]. We had no further incidents on that voyage. . .

After discharging cargo in Sydney and taking on a few hundred tons of coal from a steamer for ballast, we were towed around to Newcastle, where we waited a week or two for our turn at the loading dock and then took a full cargo (about 4,000 tons) of coal for Honolulu. We made an uneventful trip north through the islands, very few of which we saw, and arrived off Honolulu and were towed in to Brewer _[indecipherable]_ Wharf where the ship was discharged of its coal, then cleaned and loaded with sugar for New York again. The "Tillie Starbuck" made several voyages between N.Y. and Honolulu and was finally lost in a storm off the coast of South America. The crew was saved and the Capt. Curtis lived for some years in Oakland, [California] when he was captain of a small steamer taking garbage out to sea and dumping it. . .

I left the ship at Honolulu and moved ashore into a room in the house occupied by Capt. Nicholson, who was formerly mate of the "Starbuck." He had gone overland to San Francisco and by steamer to Honolulu, where he was employed as a mate on the Interisland steamers. He was finally made captain of a steamer and it was lost on the first trip, less than 100 miles from Honolulu, near Lahaina, Maui. He was fired from the Interisland Co. but was again employed as pilot by the Baldwin interests, who owned the port of Kahului before the Territory of Hawai`i took over all ports in the islands. . . He finally died in the hospital in Honolulu. . .

SECOND MATE on the 'KEAUHOU'
BRINGING a SUGAR MILL from
HONOLULU to S E Hawai`i ISLAND

After leaving the sailing ship, I got a job as second mate on the small steamer, "Keauhou," and my salary jumped from $14 a month to $45 _[indecipherable]_ a month. One of the first jobs I had was when the Keauhou had to take a complete sugar mill, which was built in St. Louis, Mo. [Missouri] . ., from Honolulu to Pahala on the southeast coast of Hawai`i. . . The mill rollers weighted ten tons and many of the other parts about as much.

As there was no harbor or wharf at Punaluu where we had to land the mill, we had to lay at anchor about ½ mile off shore and send all the machinery ashore on a scow that had been built especially for this work. As the anchorage was out in rough water, it was a difficult job to get all that machinery ashore without breaking any of it or losing it overboard. . . We had a line from the ship to the shore, held up by buoys and when the scow was loaded, we had to haul it in to shore hand over hand, along the line to a small sheltered cove, where there was a wharf and a derrick. It was taken off the scow and loaded on railroad cars and taken to the site of the mill a few miles away.

It was my job as second mate to stay on the scow and take it in and out to the landing. We had to pull through the surf at times, and several times the scow was swept by the seas, but everything was lashed down and not washed off the scow. We were wet then all the time, but the air and water was warm and we rather enjoyed it. It took us two trips to get that mill to its destination, about one month in all. Many days it was so rough that we could not work at all and many times we had to work at night as it was smoother then. The wind blows all day and dies out at night, and all the shipping of sugar from this port is done at night when the sea is smoother. One ten-ton roller was a load for the scow, and we were two weeks on each trip unloading that mill. This work was very good experience for me as in afteryears, I had lots of jobs to do like that by myself as master of other steamers.

REGULAR INTERISLAND TRADE

After finishing the trips with the sugar mill, we went back on the regular interisland trade, taking cargos of freight, lumber, cattle feed, lime, and all kinds of plantation supplies to the sugar plantations, and bringing sugar, rice and cattle back to Honolulu. When we went to the Island of Hawai`i, we always had to bring cattle on deck with a hold full of sugar in bags. The cattle were loaded at Kawaihae on the west side of Hawai`i, a smooth water port. They were taken out of the cattle pen on shore by the mounted cowboys and hauled out to the ship's boat, which was tied up to a line just where the water was too deep for the cattle to get a foothold on the bottom. The cowboys made the cattle swim out. . .to the boat, where they threw the line around the cattle's horns to the boat crew who hauled the cows alongside the boat and put on a "head line" by which they were lashed with their heads alongside the boat and then the boat was hauled out alongside the steamer and the cows hoisted on board by a sling under their belly. . . On deck they were lashed by the head rope (around the horns) to a span on the ship's rail and kept that way all the way to Honolulu. As it is almost always rough between the islands and the small steamers roll and toss around, some of the cows fall down on deck, but their heads are still lashed to the span. Part of the crew are always on watch to see that the cows are gotten up on their feet as soon as possible. One of the quickest ways to get a cow up is to twist her "stern line" (tail) but if too much of this is done, there may be a complaint from the meat co. about broken tails.

One of the best friends I had in the islands was a Mr. Alfred Carter, who was manager of the big Parker Ranch on the Island of Hawai`i. He often was a passenger with us and at one time he asked me to pick out a place at the port of Kawaihae where a steamer could get close enough to the cattle pen to lay alongside a wharf and take the cattle on board without swimming them out to the steamer and hoisting them on board. He also asked me to design a wharf for that purpose. Both of these things I did for him and the wharf was afterward built by the Territory of Hawai`i, but that was long after I had left the employ of the Interisland Co. And gone to Pearl Harbor. There were several other places where cattle were shipped but 95% of all cows came from Kawaihae.

About this time, the plantation owners were importing laborers from many parts of the world but principally from Japan and part of our job was to take the laborers out to the various plantations, where they afterward became the chief source of the field labor until they started importing Filipinos, who now are the principal source of labor for the canefields. We would carry them on deck on top of any deck cargo we might have and there were about as many women as men who were used to breed more laborers. In these days, there were only a few harbors or docks in the other islands and most of our work was done by big cargo boats called surf boats, which were hung on davits and kept swung out at all times. The boats' crews were native Hawaiians and they made fine "boat men." The crew of a boat was four men and a boat steerer who got a little more pay and was responsible for delivering the cargo safely to the landing and when taking sugar was responsible for keeping the sugar dry if possible, big tarpaulins being kept in the boats for the purpose, as many times the boats had to go and come through the surf and sometimes were overturned and the cargo lost.

WORK for WILDER STEAMSHIP COMPANY and INTERISLAND STEAM NAVIGATION CO., 1897-1913

During the years between 1897 when I started working in Hawai`i and left the "Starbuck," I was working for two steamship companies. One was the Wilder SS [Steamship] Co. and the other the Interisland Steam Navigation Co., . . .[also] referred to as the II Co. in this memoir. The Wilder Co. was absorbed by the II Co. about 1902. I was second mate, mate, and master of various vessels during the years between 1897 and 1913, when I went as pilot to Pearl Harbor. I spent three very happy years on the S.S. Hawai`i with Hilo as the home port, learning how to handle the steamer and the wire at wire landings. Our duty in those years was to act as tenders to the Matson sailing ships. There were two steamers, the Hawai`i and the Kaiulani, in this trade, and our work was to tow the sailing ships in and out of Hilo Bay and to place them at their moorings under the direction of the pilot. We then came alongside the sailing ships and took their cargo on board for the various "outside" plantations, and then brought sugar in from those plantations and delivered it to the ships to take to San Francisco.

We usually were at anchor in Hilo Bay during the nights but left each morning between 2:00 and 4:00 so as to be at the landings at daylight to start working. When necessary, we worked through all the daylight hours and such a thing as overtime was never thought of. All the plantations we worked on were within 50 miles of Hilo. In going out early in the morning, there was a mist not as thick as fog but at times obscuring the sight of the shore. We could always tell which plantation we were passing by the smell. The land breeze blows off the land during the night and each plantation had its own peculiar smell. . . we could hear the mules braying as we passed. The water was deep close to shore all along this coast and we were never very far off the rocks. . . Most of the places we went to had wire landings, but there were a few derrick landings, which were mostly disliked by the captain and crews of the steamer, as they were more dangerous in rough weather than the wire landings which could be worked in most any kind of weather except when the wind was from the north, when even they were unsafe.

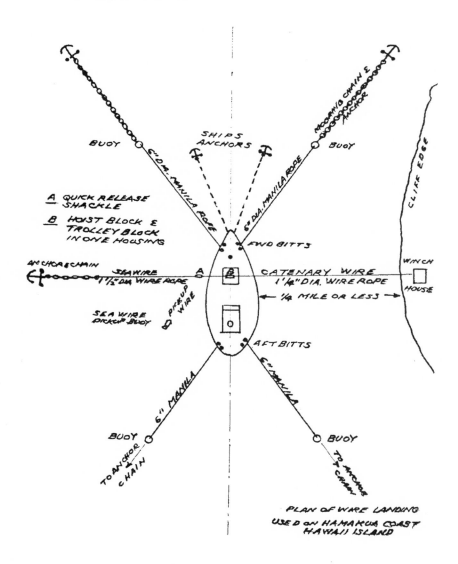

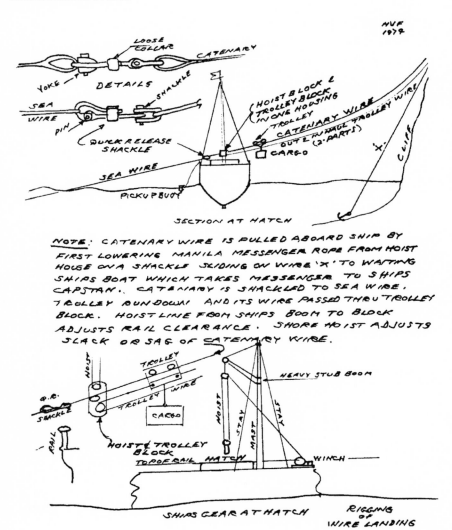

While I was mate on the Hawai`i in about the year 1901, the Captain Frank Berg suddenly left at Hilo and went up to San Francisco on one of the Matson sailing vessels. I was made captain of the Hawai`i at that time and later in 1912 was transferred to the "Helene," which ran out of Honolulu but went into Hilo sometimes to put sugar into the sailing ships or to help out the two Hilo steamers when there was too much work for them to handle.

1911 - 1912 on 'SS CLAUDINE'

About the year 1911 or 1912, I was again transferred to the "S. S. Claudine" and remained there until 1913, when I went to Pearl Harbor as pilot for the Navy. The "Claudine" made weekly trips from Honolulu to Hilo with cargo and passengers, calling at Lahaina, Kahului, Hana and Laupahoehoe on the way and the same route returning from Hilo. We left Honolulu every Friday night at 5 p.m. and returned to Honolulu on Thursday morning. Thus we had two days each week in Honolulu and one day in Hilo.

At one time before 1900, I made a trip as second mate on the "Waialeale." We went northwest from the Hawaiian Islands and called at Necker Island [Mokumanamana], French Frigate Shoals, Laysan Island, Midway and Ocean Island. We went beyond Ocean Island into east longitude, where an island had been reported, but its position was marked PD on the charts (position doubtful). Our job was to find that island or determine that it was not there. We could find no trace of it or any indication that it had ever been there. On our report, it was removed from future charts. The mate on that expedition was Capt. Wm. Foster, who later became Harbormaster at Honolulu and who later gave me the job of pilot at Honolulu after I left PH. [Pearl Harbor] The captain of the Waialele was Capt. Mosher, who afterward became pilot for Hilo.

WILDER STEAMSHIP CO., 'SS HAWAI`I' at HILO

For some months, I was purser on the "S.S. Kauai," but I did not like that job very much and left it to return to Waterbury for a visit. After a few months at home, I came back to Honolulu and resumed work for the Wilder SS Co., who at that time operated the "SS Hawaii" at Hilo. There was only a small dock at Hilo in those days and no breakwater. All ships except the II steamers had to lay at anchor with lines to stern buoys. They were moored so as to be head to the swells that always come into Hilo Bay over the reef on which the breakwater was built in later years.

The "Hawaii" had to lie alongside the sailing ships when taking freight or discharging sugar and at times it was so rough in Hilo Bay that we had to use big, thick fenders made of old, worn-out mooring lines between the ship and the steamer. When the sailing ships were loaded, we would tow them out to sea far enough for them to pick up the tradewinds which did not extend into Hilo Bay. There was a space just to windward of Mauna Loa and Mauna Kea where the wind was light and with regular land and sea breezes not connected with the tradewinds. At night it blew cold wind down off the mountains and about 8:00 or 9:00 in the morning, the sea buoys would start blowing in toward the land. There was always a lot of rain around Hilo, not steady but showers most any time during the night or day. So we had to keep tarpaulins and hatch tents handy to cover the freight and sugar during the squalls which did not last very long.

EARLY MATSON LINE

The first steamer that Captain Matson bought was called "Enterprise," and ran between San Francisco and Hilo. After he bought the second steamer, the "Hiloman," the sailing ships were gradually withdrawn and the steamer took over the trade carried on by the "Falls of Cyde," a four-mast bark.... There was also the "Amy Turner," a small bark operated by the Brewer Co. From this fleet of ships began the present "Matson Line" with the Lurline and about 30 other steamers now operating between San Francisco, Honolulu, Hilo, Kahului and Port Allen on Kauai. As the Matson ships began to call at other ports in the Hawaiian Island and the Hilo Railroad was built along the Hamakua Coast, the wire landings and derrick landings were abandoned and the interisland steamer lost so much of the business that at present there is but one small steamer, the "Humuula" operating in the islands. All of the passenger business has been taken over by the airplanes and a small portion of local freight is handled by barges towed by Young Bros. tow boats...

1902 - TOOK 'HELENE' to
SAN FRANCISCO for REPAIR

About the year 1902, I was selected to take the "Helene" up to San Francisco to be repaired. The inner frames of the hull of this steamer had been so eaten and rusted away by the acid from the fertilizer which we carried as cargo that it was feared the plates would be rusted through and the hull weakened. We took a full load of sugar to San Francisco to the "Western Sugar Refinery" and when that was discharged, I took the steamer down to the Union Ironworks to the repair dock. I did not call for a pilot for this short run and on entering the slip at the Ironworks, we ran into a mud bank as it was low tide. After a lot of work, we managed to force the steamer through the mud and get to the dock.

The next day when we got up on the drydock, we saw the marks of the mud two feet up on the ship's bottom. As we have no rise and fall of tide to think of in Honolulu (only about one foot plus minus), I forgot that there is six feet or more of rise and fall of the tide in San Francisco Bay. If I had waited till the next morning, there would have been plenty of water to get to the dock. I had my wife along on this trip, and we rented a room at the Salvation Army house on Market St. for the time we were there. After the repair work was finished, we loaded a cargo and a deck load of big log buoys and anchors and chains for the moorings at the wire landings. We returned to Honolulu with no further trouble.

1912 - TOOK 'SS KILAUEA' to SAN FRANCISCO for REPAIRS

A few years later, about 1912, I was selected again to take the "S.S. Kilauea" up to San Francisco to the Union Ironworks for repairs to her hull. She was only a few months old when they ran against some rocks on the Island of Hawai`i near South Point and while not stuck there, the hull was damaged more than could be repaired in Honolulu. As usual, we took a full load of sugar and 20 passengers besides my wife and young boy, Richard II, who was about a year old. Mr. Gedge, secretary of the Interisland Co., was one passenger. He went up to make arrangements for the repair work, and a Mr. Geo. Klugel, a friend of the Interisland Co., went along for the ride. He was also a good friend of mine. That trip was uneventful and after the repairs were finished, and a full load of freight put on board, we returned to Honolulu.

Several years after I had become a pilot for Honolulu, I used some of my accumulated vacation time to go to Galveston, Texas, at the request of the II Co., and bring back a small steamer which they had bought in Cuba. They had taken a much longer time than necessary for that voyage so as to make a few more dollars for the trip. While waiting in Galveston, I had a chance to explore around the city and see the long city wall which was constructed after the city was nearly destroyed by a hurricane and a raise of the water of the Gulf of Mexico, which killed several thousand people and did millions of dollars of damage to property. When the steamer finally did arrive at Galveston, it was put in a repair yard with a machine shop and given a complete overhaul. Mr. Gedge of the II Co. was there to supervise the transfer and Lykes Bros. were the agents for the II Co. there. When the repair work was finished, the ship was loaded with sulfur and some small amounts of other cargo.

Before we left Galveston, we had to take the ship to "Texas City" for fuel oil. That was the first time I had tied out the handling of this ship, and I found her to be the worst steering ship I had ever seen. We had to put it on the drydock and add several feet to the area of the rudder. That helped some but she never did steer properly as long as she belonged to the II Co.

TRIP to GALVESTON, PANAMA CANAL, and LOS ANGELES, CALIFORNIA

At this time, I was not working for the II Co. But was a pilot for the Territory of Hawai'i in Honolulu. I had several weeks' vacation due me and I used that for the trip to Galveston. As the trip was prolonged so much, I feared I would lose my job as pilot for I had outstayed my leave due to no fault of my own. However, my friends in Honolulu fixed it up with the Board of Harbor Commissioners so that I did not lose anything.

After leaving Galveston, I found that the ship could only make five or six knots at full speed. We had a very good chief engineer, Mr. Brown, who had been engineer on much larger ships. He had an instrument with him for measuring the work of an engine. (Indicator.) He reported to me the second day out that the low pressure cylinder was not doing any work. The engine was a small triple expansion or three-cylinder job. He took the cover plate off the L.P. valve chest and we found that the L.P. valve was all broken in many pieces and some pieces had fallen down into the condenser. The engine had been overhauled at the repair yard in Galveston, but the engineers there had not found this broken valve. This valve chest was a very peculiar one, as it had two cover plates. The outer plate had been taken off, but the inner plate which covered the sliding valve had never been removed.

The chief engineer fixed the engine to run on two cylinders and we kept on to the Panama Canal, where we had a new valve cast and installed at the government shops there. We were about a week at the Atlantic end of the Canal and I found one of the pilots there who had been a second mate with me on one of the Interisland steamers. He took me around on several trips on other steamers through the canal and returned by train, as the canal pilots only work one way through the canal. Another set of pilots from Balboa take the ship through from the Pacific end.

While waiting at Colon, I had a chance to spend one half-day in the control room of the Gaton _[indecipherable]_ Locks (a set of three locks) where all the valves, gates and guard chains are handled by one man on a model of the three locks, all by remote control.

After our repairs were finished and we passed through the canal, we went up the west coast to Los Angeles Harbor, where at Wilmington, we took fuel oil at the Union Oil docks. On the way from Panama to Los Angeles, we had one fireman take sick with what looked like appendicitis. I had the wireless operator send out a call for a doctor on any ship in the same part of the ocean. We got a reply that one of the big passenger ships was near and would alter her course to meet us. This was done and the ship's doctor came on board and he offered to take the sick man to his ship where he could be treated and operated on if he needed surgery, which was done. I afterwards heard that he was operated on and made a good recovery. We were able to make about 7-1/2 knots after the engine had been repaired. After leaving San Pedro, we were able to make a little more time with a fair wind and current. It took us 51 days to get from Galveston to Honolulu.

SEATTLE, WASHINGTON, on VACATION TIME to GET TOWBOAT for YOUNG BROTHERS

Another time I used some more accumulated vacation time to go to Seattle, Washington, to bring down a big towboat for Young

Brothers Towboat Co. The towboat company paid my way up on a Matson steamer, the old "Maui" and by train to Seattle. There I was met by Jack Young, the manager of the company, and taken to the "Arctic Club," where he had engaged a room for me. The towboat, called "Mikimiki," was nearly finished and a steel barge that Mr. Young was having built there was also nearly ready. After a trial run, we took the barge in tow and went out through the "straits" in clear weather and down to Honolulu in 15 days.

It was when in Seattle that I first me Mr. L.H. Coolidge, a naval architect, who had designed the "Mikimiki" and some other boats for Young Bros. We became very friendly and we have continued to correspond to this day. I was able to entertain him a little in Honolulu on the occasion of a later visit he made to observe the operation of the boats he had designed and built for Young Bros.

I had bought a Ford automobile in Seattle through the agents for Jack Young (Alexander and Baldwin) at a good discount. It cost me only about $400 and it, along with Jack Young's personal car, was put on the barge and covered with a big tarpaulin and lashed down to steel loops welded to the deck for that purpose. They came through in perfect condition with no water on them. The barge was also loaded with engine oil for the use of the diesel engines in all the other boats of the Young Bros. Fleet.

The engines of the "Mikimiki" were two 1050 HP Fairbanks Morris marine engines, and there were two guarantee engineers on board in addition to the regular crew. Jack Young was also on board. We had not trouble on this trip down and delivered the towboat and barge to Young Bros. safely.

WORK on the 'CLAUDINE' IN 1911 - 1912

To go back to my work with the II Co., I was transferred from the "Helene" to the "Claudine" about 1911 or 1912 and was master of that steamer for over a year. During one trip, I took my father and mother on a round trip to Hilo and up to the Volcano and a horse and buggy ride on Maui while at Kahului.

WORK at PEARL HARBOR in 1913

Early in the year 1913, I was asked to go to Pearl Harbor and be the first pilot and harbormaster after the channel was opened to navigation. The channel had been in process of being dredged out and widened for over ten years. On the formal opening, there was a parade of steamers led by the U.S. Cruiser "California" and followed by the "Claudine" and "Helene," which went in through the newly opened channel and they all anchored off the machine shop where a big celebration was held. I was on the "Helene" that time and we had a few passengers on board, including Mrs. Nelson and some friends. The "California" poked her bow into the bank on the west side of the channel ear "hospital point" but got off without any damage.

I was appointed Pilot by the Secretary of the Navy, and in the letter he said, "You will be furnished quarters in Pearl Harbor." This was never done, and I was never given anything in place of the "quarters" I should have had. They were ready to have ships taken in and out of Pearl Harbor at this time and as I was recommended by a man named McStocker, who I did not know, but who evidently knew of my work with the II Co., I was given the job at $3,000 "per annum" which I understood as meaning every day and every hour during the year. There was no such thing as working hours or overtime. I was on call at all times and was well satisfied with the conditions.

The big number one drydock had been under construction for two years. One section about 300 feet long, where they had just finished pouring the concrete for the floor by the "tremie method" of depositing concrete under water, had been destroyed the day before I arrived on the job. When they had pumped the water out of that section, the hydraulic pressure forced the whole bottom up and wrecked the whole operation. They knew it was rising as they had instruments watching it and fortunately, no one was down inside that section when it came up in a matter of a few seconds. The cause of the upward pressure was like trying to hold an empty bucket down in a tub of water. The ground all over this part of the island and particularly in Pearl Harbor, is a very porous coral formation and is full of water all the time.

During the eight years I was at Pearl Harbor, I watched the clearing out of the old excavation for the drydock and after a wait of two years, while plans for new drydock were made in Washington, I watched the construction of a new drydock, which was successfully finished and opened by the time the then Secretary of the Navy, Josephus Daniels, who came from Washington for that purpose and also to inspect the shops and installations which had been built during those years. I had some talk with him on the way down to PH [Pearl Harbor]. I had the good fortune to meet him in Mexico City in 1940 when he was U.S. Ambassador to Mexico, and I was in trouble there, having had all my money and other things stolen from our car while in a theater in Mexico City. He was very helpful and said he remembered me (which I doubt) and he instructed the counsel there to do what he could for me in the way of sending cables to Honolulu for more money and asking the police to help look for the thief. The only thing recovered was the value of the traveler's checks which were paid without question.

JAPANESE CRUISERS STATIONED in PEARL HARBOR

The years I spent as pilot in Pearl Harbor were on the whole very pleasant and most instructive in that I was a close observer of all the construction work going on there such as drydock, piers, channel improvements, ship building and machine and boiler shop machines being installed. My work as pilot took no more than ten percent of my time, so I had lots of time to wander around the Navy yard in the steam launch furnished to me, to explore the various channels and locks of PH. During the time I was there, I had many interesting experiences with vessels that came in and went out of there. During the first year I was there, there were two Japanese cruisers stationed in Hawai'i and they made their headquarters in PH. They were there supposedly for the protection of the islands, but I suspect their chief business was gathering information about Pearl Harbor and the various ports in the Hawaiian Islands. They made their base of operations the Navy yard at PH and I had to take them in and out about every two weeks. They were there about two years, and I became very well acquainted with the admiral in command and several of his officers. Before they left, they knew more about the layout of the Navy yard and conditions in Hawai'i than some of the American naval officers stationed at PH.

Among the first ships to enter PH were a couple of old Navy colliers used to carry sand from the Columbia River to PH. The reason they imported sand was that the engineer who designed the drydock blamed the poor quality of the concrete used for the floor of the drydock (that was destroyed) on the use of coral sand from the beaches of Oahu. The Columbia River sand was supposed to make a stronger concrete. These ships were docked at temporary wharves inside the excavation for the _[indecipherable]_.

130-TON FLOATING CRANE

Another interesting job was building of a 130-ton floating crane in Honolulu and its being towed to PH when it was finished. It was a risky thing to try and tow this crane with its heavy overhead structures out of Honolulu through five miles of open sea and into the PH channel. I was on the towboat as pilot and we left Honolulu at 3:00 in the morning as being less windy and rough at that time. While at sea, the crane rolled and pitched so that the overhead structure looked like the "walking beam" of a sidewheel steamer. But it did not capsize and we delivered it safely to the Navy dock in PH. This crane was later used to lift a 60-ton gun from the dock of the Matson steamer, "Wilhelmina," which I took in and out.

The steamer, "Great Northern" was used to carry U.S. soldiers to Russia and I had to take it in and out of PH channel to the "coal dock" to take on fuel oil which was stored nearby. This ship on one occasion was too light and high in the water due to her fuel oil being nearly all used up and having no cargo on board except the soldiers' baggage and supplies; that she was topheavy, and on turning in from sea to enter PH Channel, she rolled so far over that the officer in command thought she would capsize, and he ordered his soldiers off the decks and to go down below to reduce the center of gravity. It is the habit of some ships when in that condition to roll just so far over and flop from side to side, but they seldom go completely over. There were some ships of the American President line that used to set the same way while waiting for the port officials off Honolulu Harbor. When their fuel tanks are filled, they steady up and act normally.

During the first war (WWI) [World War I], while I was at PH, all the good officers of the U.S. Navy were serving on ships or on shore on the Atlantic side and only the old and least efficient officers were sent to PH.

I had been furnished with a steam launch and crew of four sailors to use as a pilot boat and to transport me to and from PH in place of giving me no quarters there. I used this steam launch to take me to and from PH every day and also to board ships needing a pilot both at PH and Honolulu. I had to _[indecipherable]_ all Navy ships in Honolulu as well as PH. The launch remained at the Navy wharf, pier 4, in Honolulu overnight.

SAILING VESSEL STUCK at ELEELE, KAUAI HELPED by NAVY TOWBOAT 'NAVAJO'

One very interesting experience was a trip I made on the navy towboat "Navajo" to tow a sailing ship to Honolulu during a very severe Kona or S.E. storm. The sea was very rough and a sailing vessel had drifted in so close to the shore at Eleele, Kauai, now Port Allen, that its stern was hitting the rocks and the rudder was jammed "hard over" and could not be moved. Eleele was on the southwest shore of the Island of Kauai and the wind and sea were from south to southeast. There were no towboats at that place, but the "S.S. Kukui," the island lighthouse tender, was somewhere around the island, and was called to come to the help of the ship. She got a line on board the ship and hauled her away from the rocks until the anchors had been hove up and then steamed out to sea with the ship. The lighthouse tender sent a wireless message to the Navy at PH requesting help as she had no proper towing gear and would not be able to hold onto the ship much longer. She was able to tow the ship far enough out from the land so that in case the towing line broke, she would not drift back on shore.

The Navy towboat, "Navajo," was made ready and a spare towing hawser put on board. I was sent on board to assist the regular captain of the towboat, who did not know much about towing or about the coasts or harbors around the islands and in addition was very seasick as soon as we got outside the PH channel. We started out from PH at about 10 p.m. in the very middle of the storm and had no sooner gotten out of the channel than the brickwork in the steam boiler (in the firebox) fell down due to the heavy pitching and rolling that we did as soon as we were out of the quiet water in the channel. We kept on going and at daylight the next morning, we found the ship floating alone but with the lighthouse tender standing by, as her towing line had parted and they could not get another line on board. The captain and most of the crew of the "Navajo" were seasick but I managed to get enough men on deck to handle the towline and we got a towline on board the ship. We started toward Honolulu slowly, as the ship could not steer and was always away off on the towboat quarter instead of right astern.

BAD 'KONA' STORMS

After many hours and one broken towline, we arrived off Honolulu, but it was too rough to enter port with an unmanageable ship. I took the ship around the Island of Oahu into smooth water on the north side. We kept towing around slowly waiting for word that it was safe to enter. We finally went back around the island to Honolulu, and with the help of a small towboat to steer the ship, we got it safely into the dock. That was one of the worst "Kona storms" I ever saw. However, I was out in one nearly as bad in the "Helene" before I went to Pearl Harbor. That time we left Honolulu with a full load of freight and a big dock load as usual. It was blowing from the southeast so we left port at 5 p.m. and it gradually got worse so that we could make no headway on our course to Maui but had to steam slowly head to the sea all night. In the morning we were still in sight of Diamond Head Light and not many miles from Honolulu. We lost one boat during the night, washed out of the divots, and some of the deck load of lumber. It got a little bettr the next day and we started for Maui and waited there for the storm to die out enough for us to continue on our way.

These "Kona storms" or southeast gales are the worst kind of weather we have in Hawai'i and they occur in wintertime from about December to March. Some years there are several of these storms alternating with calm spells and other years there are no SE storms at all, with the tradewinds blowing all winter with many calm days. During the summer, the NE wind blows constantly from NE to ENE, sometimes strong and at other times moderate. I have noticed that the strong spells of wind correspond to the days of full moon. What connection there is between the moon and the strength of the wind, I do not know.

SIX MONTHS to RETIREMENT from PEARL HARBOR

After I left PH and went to work in Honolulu, I still did whatever piloting was necessary at PH until they could get another pilot to take my place. This was about six months until Capt. Otterson was persuaded to take the job, which he held for many years through the second [world] war, when there were about 20 pilots employed at PH under Capt Otterson as chief pilot. A lot of these wartime pilots were Navy officers and did not know very much about handling ships.

Several times after I left PH, when the Navy sent a fleet of ships down for exercises around the islands, I was asked to come down and help out with the piloting as Capt. Otterson could not handle so many ships by himself. He was alone at those times. Sometimes there were as many as 140 ships of all kinds in the "fleet." All of these ships did not need pilots, but the battleships and cruisers all asked for pilots, while most of the smaller vessels like destroyers and towboats either came in by themselves or were guided in by other local Navy men (not pilots) who knew something about the channel and navy Yard berths.

REASON for LEAVING PEARL HARBOR

The reason I left PH was a new young officer who was acting "Captain of the Yard." He told me I could not use the steam launch to take me back and forth to Honolulu and that I would have to stay around the Yard until 4 p.m. like any other working man. As I was paid a "per annum" salary, I considered my time as available at any time any day or night for piloting and was always there when I had something to do. When I was told to keep regular hours, I sat right down and wrote out my resignation and left as soon as I got the job as pilot for Honolulu. There were not many vessels going to PH at that time, so it was not hard to handle both jobs until Capt. Otterson came there. If there came a turn for me at Honolulu while I was doing a job for PH, one of the other pilots in Honolulu took care of that job for me.

VIEW of APPROACHES to HONOLULU HARBOR from HOME at PUNCHBOWL

The work at Honolulu was very pleasant and was the kind of work I liked. The pilots were subject to call at any time day or night and a large part of the work was done at night. Many of the big passenger ships set the sailing time for midnight so as to allow the passengers time for an evening at the hotels before leaving. We did not have any set hours for working and when not doing pilot work, we were allowed to be at home but subject to call by telephone any time. As I lived on the hillside and had a good view of the approaches to Honolulu Harbor, I could often see the ships coming from the west before the lookout man in the tower. From the east my view was not so good, and I could not see as far as Diamond Head. We had two watchmen on duty at all times. One man lived in a Government house at Diamond Head and he reported all ships from the east (and west also). He lived there and was on duty 24 hours a day, being relieved at times to go to town when necessary. The other two watchmen stood 12-hour watches in the top of the Aloha Tower, where the pilot's office was. They had the duty of getting the pilots down to the office on time (by telephone) and keeping the pilots informed as to sailing times of ships not on scheduled regular times of sailing.

OFFICE at ALOHA TOWER

As my home was on a hillside, I always backed my automobile into the garage stern first, and I had a small incline made of planks under the rear wheels so I could always jump into the car and by releasing the brakes, the car would roll down the incline, and I always could get it started even if the battery was weak or run down. If there was plenty of time, I often walked down to the Aloha Tower about one mile and I could do it easily in 15 minutes. In the car, it took less than five minutes at the most. Our office was on the 10th floor of Aloha Tower, 198 feet high, and there was an elevator worked by push button so anyone could use it. The lower floors were occupied by the Harbormaster's office and various other government departments. There were ten floors in that tower and in later years, we had the use of the fourth floor as our office.

One thing that would occur in no other place than up in an airplane was the sight of a rainbow with a complete circle seen from the top of the tower. This could be seen only under certain conditions of sunshine and mist or light rain when the sun was low in the east early in the morning. I have seen this many times from the tower.

The pilots were allowed two weeks' vacation each year and this could be left to accumulate for as many years as desired. As my work as pilot was very easy–almost like a continuous vacation–I never took a vacation unless I had an offer of a job to bring some vessel from the mainland to Honolulu or when I wanted to make a trip to the mainland for my own purpose. So I usually had plenty of accumulated leave ready to be taken when the opportunity came to use it.

TRIP in 1934 to SAN FRANCISCO, PANAMA CANAL, NEW YORK

One trip I took I think was around 1934. I got permission from the Army Transport Service to go on the "S.S. Chateau Thierry" from Honolulu to Brooklyn, N.Y. by paying one dollar per day for my food. We went to San Francisco first and then down the West Coast to the Panama Canal and up the Atlantic side to N.Y. We were docked at the U.S. Army dock at S. Brooklyn just across from Staten Island. Bob Carmichael came over in his car and took me to Jersey City, where I lived for a few days, sleeping at the YMCA and eating with the family. I bought a Ford car and later took my trunk up to Cold Spring and remained there for the rest of my stay with various trips to points of interest. When my time was nearly up, I started back to Honolulu via San Francisco and stopped at various national parks along the way. I shipped the car to Honolulu on a Matson steamer and returned to work after about 3 months of vacation.

There are many details of my life in Hawai`i that I have omitted from these notes, such as the several trips my mother and father made to Honolulu before they sold their home in Waterbury and moved to Honolulu, where they lived in a cottage alongside our house until my father died and my mother moved back to her old house in Cold Spring. The arrival and bringing up of our family of three children and their growing old enough to get married and establish homes of their own. The arrival of grandchildren and my retirement from the pilot service in 1939.

***

JOURNAL of TRAVELS and 'TRAILER-ING'

The following is a condensed account of our travels from 1936 to the present time. The detailed day by day account of our travels with the trailer is contained in another volume.[1]

In 1936, after my son Julian had recovered from an appendix operation, I arranged for him and his mother to make a trip to the mainland. I wrote to my friend, Mr. Coolidge in Seattle to look for a trailer and have it ready. . .when they arrived. They left Honolulu about 9/1/36 on the "Ararangi" and went to Vancouver, BC [British Columbia, Canada]. Mrs. Cunningham, a friend of the family, went along with them. They took the Ford car with them. From Vancouver they went in the Ford car to Seattle to the home of Mr. Coolidge. . .[who had] picked out a trailer for them, . . .waiting for them to approve of it before buying it. They finally got started away from Seattle with the trailer and after that they traveled for several months, and going as far west as Carlsbad Caverns in NM [New Mexico] and finally landing in San Francisco just in time to get held up by the strike of seamen that held all American ships from sailing on the Pacific Ocean. They spent the winter at the Miriam Auto Court on Miriam St., Daly City. It was a very cold winter with snow at times. I had just arranged for them to return on a Japanese steamer by paying the $200 fine which was levied against any foreign ship carrying passengers between American ports when the strike ended and they returned by a Matson steamer. They left the car and trailer in storage in SF [San Francisco] and I later sold the Ford as part payment on a new Studebaker. The trailer they used was a "Silver Dome" with wood frame, no dolly and no brakes. It must have been in pretty good condition for it gave them no trouble and was easily towed by the Ford.

TRAVELS with FRANCES

In 1937 I planned a trip to the Coast and back to New York, using the trailer and taking Frances with me. Her employer, Mr. Fred Ohrt, manager of Honolulu Board of Water Supply where she was working very kindly gave her 3 months leave.[2] I had 3 months of accumulated leave so we left Honolulu on the Lurline in the latter part of April

1937. I had arranged to pick up a Studebaker in SF so did not take any car with me from Honolulu. On the same steamer went H. V. Frazier, whom she knew at Board of Water Supply and who was an engineer there and would afterward become her husband.

We landed in SF and went to the Stewart Hotel on Geary St., where she remained while I went to the Studebaker agent to get the car and have it fitted with a towing rig. I also had the trailer taken out of storage on Mason St. and taken to the Studebaker shop to be fitted to the car. We got everything assembled and tested out and then went to Golden Gate Auto Court on Mission St. in Calma to spend the night and get organized for the trip. We started early on May 2 and went to Yosemite. While there we met Mr. and Mrs. Spare from Honolulu while at Glacier Point. There was still plenty of snow around, but it was not cold. After leaving the park, we went south and east through Arizona, NM, and stopped at Carlsbad Caverns after leaving El Paso, Tx. [Texas]

We went down to Laredo, Tx., and into Mexico. We went as far as Victoria and left the trailer there while we went into Mexico City in the car alone. We were two days in Mexico City and then returned to Victoria, hooked on the trailer and returned to Laredo. From Laredo we went northeast, crossing the states on the most direct line to South Bend, Ind. [Indiana], where the Studebaker cars were made and where I was going to have heavier springs installed on the car. While there waiting for the work to be done, I saw a "Pierce Arrow" trailer standing on the floor of a dealer showroom. It was for sale cheap, so I traded in the Silver Dome trailer and took the new one, which has hydraulic brakes and a steel frame covered with aluminum. I paid $520 cash and traded in the old trailer. I had to have the car fitted with a control for the trailer brakes and I sold the stove out of the Pierce Arrow to make more room inside. The brake system worked very satisfactorily as long as I had it and was only replaced by electric brakes when I had a new axle installed under the trailer in Los Angeles some years later.

From South Bend we went east along the south shore of Lake Erie to Niagara Falls and from there through New York State to Cold Spring. We remained at Cold Spring a few weeks and from there made a side trip with the trailer up the Hudson River to Montreal and Quebec, across the _[indecipherable]_ Bridge to the south side of the St. Lawrence River and out to Gaspe, back through Maine to Cold Spring, all in one week. The roads to and from the Gaspe were gravel and rough and very steep grades in some places. One grade in particular I remember going down into the town of Gaspe; it was so steep that I am sure I would not have made it if we were going the other way. After a few more days at Cold Spring, we started for home via Jersey City and the Lincoln Highway, which joins U.S. 30 nearly all the way to Yellowstone Park. We left US 30 at Rock Springs, Wyo. [Wyoming] and went to Teton National Park via Jackson Hole and Hogback Canyon. From Teton we went to Yellowstone and remained long enough to see what we could from the highways.

Leaving Yellowstone from the northern entrance, we went north through Great Falls and Helena to Glacier National Park. There we camped at a campground on the east side of St. Mary's Lake and made side trips over all the available roads on that side. Frances took a two-day horseback trip with a guide and several others over the mountains to the west side and I took the trailer over there and met her at the hotel there. I went over Logan Pass and down the west side to Lake McDonald. From Glacier we went down by Flathead Lake to No. 10 highway near Missoula. Then west through Idaho to Spokane, WA and Coulee Dam. Over Snoqualmie Pass to Seattle where we camped while we visited the Coolidges. We made a 2-day trip with Mr. Coolidge as a guide to Skagit Power House and a ride on the lake behind the Diablo Dam on a passenger launch he had designed. After going up to Mt. Rainier, we left Seattle and went up along the Hood Canal and around the Olympic Peninsula, stopping one night at the state park on Lake Crescent. Then down the Oregon Coast Highway after going up the Columbia River on the WA side to Hood River Bridge and down the Oregon side to Portland. . .

***

NOTES

2 - FATHER'S SEA LIFE, MOTHER'S MOTHER

1. See feature included at the end of this book: Special Addition: "The Diary and Ships' Log" (Condensed) by Richard Nelson.

6 - LIFE TOGETHER AS PARENTS

1. On November 19, 1975, an earthquake occurred off the coast Hawai`i island. The thirty-two campers at Halape Beach Park were reported to have rushed toward the ocean because of rock fall from the cliff and earth movement. Two waves generated by the quake–5', and then 26' high–washed the unfortunate campers into a ditch area near the cliff base. In that ordeal, two campers died and nineteen suffered injuries. [Information gathered from www.pdc.org/iweb/tsunami_history.jsp Sources: National Geophysical Center; Pacific Tsunami Museum Archives; Tsunami, University of Washington]

2. The Piko (Summit) Club was a hiking and trail club founded on O`ahu for the purpose of defense reconnaissance in 1931 by two hiking enthusiasts, Hawai`i-born Territorial Forester Charles S. Judd and newcomer Major General Briant H. Wells, commander of the Hawaiian Division at Schofield Barracks. For some years, men, only, were admitted. At first, it was strictly officers and enlisted men; membership requirements included crossing the Ko`olau and/or Wai`anae ranges three times on foot. In time, the membership was extended to civilians for the purposes of fitness and liaison. This exploration also resulted in much of the established trail network of the Island of O`ahu and a solution to the wild pig problem via hunters using those trails.

When the author's co-worker, geologist Chester Wentworth from the Board of Water Supply, invited her along, this was a testimony to Wentworth's belief in her strength and endurance, and a vote cast for her appreciation of such outdoor pursuits. By this time, the Sunday hikes were reportedly topped off by social occasions attended by women and children and occasional overnights in forestry cabins or private homes. [See *The Piko Club: Hiking Oʻahu in the 1930s*, by Stuart M. Ball, Jr., author of three Hawaiʻi guide books. Portions of *The Piko Club* were published in the Hawaiian Journal of History, vol. 37 (2003).]

8 - MY *KUMU*, MARY KAWENA PUKUI

1. Pele, or Madam Pele, is the name given the volcano goddess, "she" who creates and destroys land throughout Polynesia. The goddess Pele represents the great geophysical power that forces its way out of undersea Pacific plates. Volcanic fire was a phenomenon witnessed by early navigators and island settlers through earth building, or "birthing" displays of eruption resulting in volcanic islands (such as throughout the Hawaiian chain of islands), whereas earth destruction was seen to occur when rivers of hot magma and explosions of lava and ash decimated existent land and its flora and fauna.

2. The tsunami "alert" in this memoir might have been downgraded to warnings of dangerous ocean conditions for a time, with no monster wave reaching the islands, as sometimes happens–like a "temper fit" of the volcano goddess Pele that is not played out in its extreme. Exact dates have receded in the author's memory like the backwash from these waves. The 1952 tsunami, a 1957 tsunami (that did not take lives but caused enormous property damage, scoured beaches and moved road pavement), or the 1960 tsunami may relate to the author's story of Peter Black.

While they are rare, 20th century tsunamis generated by far-away earthquakes have accounted for more lost lives in Hawaiʻi than the total of all other local disasters, with most deaths occurring on the Big Island of Hawaiʻi, in 1946 and 1960. [For more information, see www.pdc.org/iweb/tsunami_history.jsp or check the sources from which the history posted on the website derives: National Geophysical Center; Pacific Tsunami Museum Archives; Tsunami, University of Washington.]

9 - RIDING a NEW PATH

1. See Section *`elima* / five, Et Cetera: From the Papers of Frances
N. Frazier: Kenneth P. Emory's August 15, 1972, "To Whom It May
Concern" letter listing the author's contributions as a translator of
the Hawaiian language.

10 - COMINGS and GOINGS

1. TEAL, forerunner of Air New Zealand, operated a total of five Solent
flying boats between 1949 and 1960 on the Coral Route connecting
South Pacific Islands to New Zealand; name changed Apr. 1, 1965.

12 - DAILY LIFE in DACCA

1. The new nation of Pakistan created in August 1947, when India
won its independence from the British, was comprised of two
geographically and culturally separated areas, one in the east, and
one in the west of India. The eastern zone (modern-day Bangladesh),
at first "East Bengal," later became East Pakistan. It was widely
perceived that West Pakistan dominated politically and exploited
the East economically, leading to many grievances and an eventual
civil war. The Bangladesh Liberation War started on March 26, 1971,
and ended on December 16, 1971.

2. In August 1947, the Partition of British India, which included
India and Burma, gave way to two new states named Pakistan and
India. Areas containing a Muslim majority (the provinces of Punjab,
Sindh, Baluchistan and the North-West Frontier) became Pakistan;
areas of Hindu and non-Muslim majority states became India, later
pronounced to be a secular country with equal rights to citizens of all
religions. [Source, "The Partition of India," Shirin Keen, Engl. Dept.,
Emory Univ., GA]

14 - FURTHER TRAVELS

1. Royal Chitwan National Park.

2. Mecca is written as Makka, with a double "k" in classical Arabic. [Ed. is indebted to Fernando Peñalosa, Professor Emeritus, retired, and author and publisher of books in a number of fields, for the information on Arabic language.]

15 - LETTER from DACCA

1. Some facts of later memoir writings were "downsized" from the full versions the author typed out to record her experiences and impressions while abroad. Letters such as this one, published in its entirety, were typed on aerogram style (lightweight) paper with carbon copies kept with the author's papers.

The originals were often sent to daughter Stephanie with similar request to the following one (date missing) : "Dear Steph, Please start this letter on its way after you and Doug have read it." There followed this alphabetized list of friends and associates (and their addresses) who would be interested in the news as it made the rounds: Mrs. Temple Bazett, Mr. and Mrs. David Greig, Mr. and Mrs. Colin Herrick, Mr. and Mrs. Drury Melone, Mrs. Patsy Metcalf, Mr. and Mrs. Robert Ray, Mr. and Mrs. John Truhan, Mr. and Mrs. Elmer Williamson (c/o of the Bishop Museum), Mr. and Mrs. Sanford Zalburg.

2. Lt. Col. John Masters, DSO, (1914-1983), an English officer in the British Indian Army and novelist, whose works are known for their treatment of the British Empire in India.

3. A time of prayers dedicated to the Goddess Durga.

17 - *ALOHA `OE* on the ORIENT EXPRESS

1. The Indo-Pakistani War of 1965, also known as the Second Kashmir War (the First having been fought in 1947), was the culmination of one of the skirmishes that took place between India and Pakistan over a border dispute between April and September of 1965. Thousands of lives on both sides were lost during those six months, and more forces were amassed in Kashmir than at any time since 1947. The war

ended with a United Nations mandated ceasefire and issuance of the Tashkent Declaration.

2. The Bangladesh Liberation War, March 26 - December 16, 1971.

3. Prince Philip, the Duke of Edinburgh, Consort to Queen Elizabeth II.

4. United States Agency for International Development, the independent federal government organization responsible for most non-military foreign aid. USAID receives overall foreign policy guidance from the U.S. Secretary of State and seeks "to extend a helping hand to those people overseas struggling to make a better life, recover from a disaster or striving to live in a free and democratic country."

5. The governing situation was the Six-Day War (June 5-10, 1967), a war between the Israeli army and armies of neighboring states (Egypt, Jordan, Syria). Other Arab states also contributed troops and arms. Since in this war Israel gained control of the Sinai peninsula, Gaza Strip, West Bank, East Jerusalem, and Golan Heights, the results affect the geopolitics of the region today. [See more, including conflicting opinions, on Wikipedia, "Six-Day War."]

19 – COURT CASES

1. Reproduced in Section `elima / five, ET CETERA from the Papers of Frances N. Frazier, is Zelie D. Sherwood's Letter of May 28, 1969. (Besides her translations, Sherwood authored *Beginner's Hawaiian*.)

20 – My STINT at the HAWAI`I STATE ARCHIVES, HONOLULU

1. The Hawai`i State Archives, located in the Kekāuluohi Building, `Iolani Palace Grounds, 364 King Street, Honolulu, HI 96813. Among other services, the research services available are searching of archives, court records, genealogy, legislative and land records, and a library and map catalog.

21 - The STORY behind the BOOK, *KALUAIKOOLAU*

1. The term "leper" is used here not deprecatingly, but in historical context. Leprosy and leper were the terms in use at the time the events of this story unfolded, before the current name, Hansen's disease, which we now know is treatable.

2. Reproduced in Section `*elima* / five, ET CETERA from The Papers of Frances N. Frazier, is the text of this talk, "Profiles of Courage."

23 - ANOTHER BOOK: *KAMEHAMEHA'S WARRIOR*, KEKŪHAUPI`O

1. Sanford Zalburg (d. 2008), writer, editor, and author of *A Spark is Struck*, is well-remembered in Hawai`i. His memorial service was reported in the February 21, 2008, issue of the Honolulu Star Bulletin, where he held the post of City Editor for many years.

2. The first edition of *Kamehameha and His Warrior Kekūhaupi`o* was published in 2000 by Kamehameha School, Bernice Pauahi Bishop Estate, Honolulu, HI.

25 - LEARNING to COPE

1. Harold Victor Frazier died on March 15, 2004. A celebration of his life was held in Līhu`e, Kaua`i, on July 29, 2004–the ninety-second anniversary of his birth (July 29, 1912).

`*elima* / five ET CETERA from
THE PAPERS of FRANCES N. FRAZIER

LETTER to my NEPHEW, July 10, 1997

1. Married to Allan Nelson, son of Julian Nelson and Evelyn (Yap) Nelson.

2. The author's younger brother.

3. The author's grandnephew, son of Allan Nelson and Cindy Nelson.

LETTER to the FORUM, September 18, 1999

1. The author wrote many open letters on various land issues and related subjects that were published in *The Garden Island*, Kaua`i Publishing Company, Lihu`e, during the time she and her husband lived on Kaua`i, raising public awareness about controlled growth and environment. The Sierra Club–Kaua`i Chapter awarded her their honorific *Pono* Award (Award for Correct or Proper Procedure). Former Mayor Edward Malapit is quoted as saying, 'Frances was known for her sassy letters to the editor of *The Garden Island*, the local Kaua`i newspaper.' (Information and archives, www.thegardenisland. com)

JACK LONDON SOCIETY SYMPOSIUM PAPER, 'PROFILE of COURAGE'

1. The sixth Biennial Symposium of the Jack London Society, sponsored by the Kaua`i Historical Society, began on October 10, 2002, at the (then) Radisson Kaua`i Beach Hotel, Lihu`e, where the author, translator of "The True Story of Kaluaiko`olau," and other local residents spoke by invitation on various aspects London's writing and life. Among these were John Lydgate, President of the Kaua`i Historical Society and grandson of the Rev. John Lydgate, whose family hosted London during his 1915 stay on Kaua`i, and Chris Cook, editor of The Garden Island newspaper. Visiting scholars also spoke at the conference.

2. Herbert "Bert" Stolz, son of Deputy Sheriff Louis Stolz of Waimea, who was killed in Kalalau Valley in June, 1893, is said to have told the story of "Koolau the Leper" to Jack London during the sail of London's yacht, the "Snark," from Oakland to Honolulu in 1906. London wrote a fictional short story with Kaluaiko`olau as a main character in his Hawaiian tales book, *House of Pride*.

`eono / six - The DIARY and SHIPS' LOG of RICHARD NELSON

1. No longer in existence.

2. Any disparities in information are left "as is."

OTHER BOOKS of INTEREST
from TropicBird PRESS
(A 1-Woman Bibliophile Company)

For readers who have enjoyed *HALI'A of HAWAI'I, A Legacy of Language*, by Frances N. Frazier:

BEHOLD KAUA'I ~ Modern Days, Ancient Ways, © 2005 Dawn Fraser Kawahara

> ISBN 1-4208-2287-X (Paperback - 6 x9", 118 pp.)
> ISBN 1-4208-2286-1 (Hardcover with dust
> jacket - 6-¼ x 9-¼", 118 pp.)

Note: *Nominated for the Hawai'i Book Publishers Assoc. Ka Palapala Po'okela (Excellent Manuscript/ Best Book) Awards 2006, contender in "Design" and "Content" award categories. The author is the winner of the James Vaughan Poetry Prize, 2002, Hawai'i Pacific Univ., and has received numerous awards from the National Federation of State Poetry Societies.*

Poems of Kaua'i with cultural and historical perspectives:

This book invites you to an island described by many as paradise. *Behold Kaua'i* is designed to bring you lasting enjoyment and insight through the poet-storyteller's eyes, and a sense of this far-flung and ancient island in modern times and from a Hawaiian cultural and historical perspective.

Behold Kaua'i is not meant to be read in one sitting, but savored as one savors and enjoys a special friend or lover, or a favorite place in which to dream and renew. As with a best friend or love who remains constant and vital, it is hoped that your initial encounter and many return engagements deepen and intensify your experience with this collection of sensitive and sensuous poems and descriptive notes.

*A book for readers who feel connection with
the earth– earth energy, bounty and beauty–
islands, and the cultures of First People.*

JACKALS' WEDDING, A Memoir of a Childhood in British India,
© 2002 Dawn Fraser Kawahara
ISBN 1-4033-4303-9 - (Paperback - 6 x 9, 558 pp.)

Note: *"Better than Fiction!"– A winner in the Writers' Digest International Self-Published Books Competition 2003, Life Stories category.*

A Travel Tale of returning to a far country of birth and first upbringing–British India–and the memories and family mysteries evoked:

"In reading *Jackals' Wedding,* I was quite overwhelmed. . . Each sentence, each paragraph drew the reader on to what was going to happen, and into the author's quest."

– Edward Farley, Prof. Of Theology, Vanderbilt University
Author, *Deep Symbols, Good and Evil, Faith and Beauty* and other books.

"Through her talent for evoking the multisensory experience, the author invites us into the world of her childhood. . . I highly recommend this book to anyone who wishes to expand their understanding of differences in cultures while finding, at the deepest levels, the commonality of human experience. I couldn't put this book down."

– Nancy Margulies, "Mindscaping" consultant, Author,
MindMapping, Leadership and the New Science, Mapping Inner Space.
With Fritjof Capra, *The Web of Life,* and other works.

Judged a good book club selection
as well as a fascinating read by readers world-wide,
who await memoir II (work in progress)
about the author's Burma & Australia experiences.

For further information or to request advance notice of upcoming books:

TropicBird Press
5753 Noni Street
Kapa`a, HI 96746-9659
U.S.A.
www.tropicbirdpress.net

ABOUT the AUTHOR and her BOOK

FRANCES N. 'HALI'A' FRAZIER, a student of Mary Kawena Pukui and Samuel Elbert, has translated numerous works for the Bishop Museum and the Hawai`i State Archives. Her most recent book, *The True Story of Kaluaikoolau as Told by His Wife, Piilani,* translated from the Hawaiian language, was published in English and Hawaiian by the Kaua`i Historical Society, Līhu`e, Kaua`i, Hawai`i (Distributed by University of Hawai`i Press, Honolulu, Hawai`i).

Anne E. O'Malley

Frances Frazier, the woman who is a Living Treasure, has lived an amazing ninety-five years to the date of first publication of her life story, a life that began fourteen years after Hawai`i became a Territory of the United States of America, and in 2009, encompasses the commemoration of fifty years of Statehood. During this long and bountiful life span we move from sailing ships through "flying boats" to jet airplanes in sequence, along with Frances' stories of her sea captain father and portions of his own nautical story embedded at the end of hers; we learn how life events led her to discovery of the Hawaiian language, a blood legacy, and how she became adept at translation and left her own legacy of important work.

*Hali`a, A Legacy of Language* is an account of a *pono* life of trust in its many decades as they unfolded, bringing her an important work to be done here in Hawai`i that became entwined with her interest in learning and correctly translating the Hawaiian language, especially as it related to land deeds that could influence the making and breaking of rights to the `āina, the land, for people of Hawaiian heritage.

Through this memoir we also hear impressions of an earlier, more gentle time on O'ahu, and work, marriage and family life set before and after the traumatic events of Pearl Harbor and World War II. We learn of the joy of an inquiring mind expanding and questioning with the opportunities that came for travel and residency abroad, and resultant contrast and comparison with home and different cultural ways in Hawai'i.

The individuality of "Aunty Hali'a's" life story–an 'olelo reflecting the experiences of one daughter of Hawai'i–by its very individuality, offers a universal connection with people, their sensibilities, and places around the globe. All of these parts merge in the telling of the serendipity of that journey, a journey as exciting as the journeys that brought her master mariner father Richard Nelson to Hawai'i at an earlier time, published in the included bonus of a special addition to his daughter's memoir.

Distributed in Hawai'i by TropicBird Press
Wailua, Kaua'i, Hawai'i

Breinigsville, PA USA
07 April 2010
235697BV00001B/5/P